Answering the Call of the Camino de Santiago

APPRECIATING THE BEAUTY
THROUGH THE CHALLENGES

Barbara Gilmore

Contact information:
Email: barbaragilmore0@gmail.com
Facebook: @AuthorBarbaraGilmore

Answering the Call of the Camino de Santiago /
Barbara Gilmore. —1st ed.

ISBN 978-0-9995912-0-8

Contents

DEDICATION

This book is dedicated to my 93 year-old, fiercely independent mother, MJ.

Thank you for the tough love.

The Why and The How

I can't recall exactly when or how I learned about the Camino de Santiago. I do know, unlike many fellow Americans who knew about the historical pilgrimage, it wasn't from seeing the movie *The Way* with Martin Sheen and Emilio Estevez. Seeing the movie would come much later.

It was more than a few years prior to my pilgrimage, I do remember, since I spent a couple of years learning everything I could about the Camino de Santiago. I became fascinated with the idea of walking the Camino, something I soon discovered that people have been doing for hundreds of years.

The more I learned about the Camino, as it is commonly known, the more I was drawn to it. I researched and read everything I could, considered a possible budget, watched airfares, mulled over the best time for me to go, and yet made no immediate plans. At least not until October 2015 after watching Oprah Winfrey's "Belief" series.

The beautifully filmed, 7-segment series explored the beliefs of people from different parts of the world, celebrating their customs, traditions, and religions.

It was the sixth episode that profiled a man from Great Britain who was about to embark on the 500-mile pilgrimage that finally convinced me. The visuals of the Camino were incredible. The episode brought to life the many photos I had seen through research. I watched that episode numerous times, and after a while, I knew I would do it. People who have walked the Camino often say it calls to you, and I don't doubt it. I became consumed with the idea of the adventure, so I guess the Camino de Santiago did call me.

There was something about the Camino de Santiago that fit into my idea of a perfect vacation. I travel often, but my 'normal' getaways usually consist of visiting my mother in Alabama or my daughter and siblings in Chicago, both places I enjoy immensely. I am grateful to be attached to the Alabama land that my grandfather farmed. He worked hard, took pride in owning land and being a viable member of his community. And when my mother retired from health services in Chicago and moved back to where she was born, I promised I would always be a part of the place that holds so much of my family's history. As for Chicago, it is where I was born, where I grew up and where I raised my daughter. My siblings still live there, so it is equally meaningful. It is never a problem for me to hop on a plane and travel to either place to spend some quality time with family. Yet, I consider neither Chicago nor Alabama a vacation spot. I consider both places home. At the time I was thinking about the Camino, I needed a vacation badly. I wanted something new, and I wanted something adventurous.

As an educator, I am afforded extended time to get away. I could do the Camino in parts, during spring break in April, or I could do the whole 500 miles (800k) during the summer months.

Making the decision to do the Camino was one thing, but putting everything in place to make it happen was a different thing altogether. I'm single, so there was only me. Though there were friends, loved ones, and colleagues who I knew were concerned about me wanting to do the solo hike, but the guilt of leaving someone behind to travel abroad for five-plus weeks did not exist. I had one 'small' problem. His name was Peter.

A little over a year ago, I agreed to take in a dog, Peter, whose previous owner no longer wanted him. He arrived as uncertain about me as I was about him. I grew up with dogs. I don't remember not having dogs around. They were either guard dogs or a source of income. They all slept in the basement, and during the day roamed the large backyard terrorizing neighbors and anyone outside the immediate family who tried to enter our domain. They were never personal.

After a short period of adjustment, Peter became personal. He became family and a roommate. I loved him almost immediately. I wanted only the best for him, and determining who would care for him for the five weeks I was planning to spend on the Camino told a toll on me. I was worried. Who would love him as I do? Would he be mistreated? Should I leave him at all? Peter was my number one dilemma.

I never once considered walking the Camino during my Christmas vacation because of snowy conditions and the seasonal closure of many albergues. Enduring the extreme heat of August was also out of the question. Realistically, July and August were ideal times to do the Camino, but if I stood a chance of completing this journey, I needed the best weather conditions possible. But when?

The school year was scheduled to end on June 16. If I left shortly after, I would finish the Camino mid-August, during the hottest and most popular time on the Camino. Maybe that time wasn't a good idea.

The calling to walk the Camino was too strong and it would not leave me. Everyday I thought about it and everyday I wondered what it would be like to walk, meet people from all over the world, visit a new part of the world, be a part of something people have been doing for thousands of years, and experience something – that in the deepest part of my soul – I knew would change me. I decided to move beyond the mere thought of doing the Camino and work on making it a reality.

Let me just say that the thought of embarking on an adventurous vacation had been swimming in my head for more than fifteen years. Originally, I had thought about climbing Mt. Everest, the ultimate, real-deal badass adventure; a 19,000-ft climb in about 30 days, at the cost of somewhere in the range $75,000, give or take 10 or 20,000 thousand. In the same manner that I researched obsessively about the Camino, I learned all I could about Mt. Everest. Essentially, the cost, frigid weather conditions, and impending danger kept Everest in the dream phase. I knew Everest wasn't for me, but the idea of it was – and still is – fascinating just the same.

I needed to decide what would be a reasonable amount of time to hike the Camino. Would I need 40 days? 50? My research about the Camino led me to John Brierley's *A Pilgrim's Guide To The Camino de Santiago*, one of the more popular guides for Americans hiking the Camino. Could I follow Brierley's suggested 33-day hiking plan? I was in reasonably good shape. I walked and hiked regularly, averaging 35-50 miles a week, so 33 days seemed realistic, making the Camino doable.

The Preparation

Things began to fall into place in January after I booked my flight to Spain. I had purchased my backpack from REI, thankfully on sale for $125. I returned the first backpack I purchased; it was an REI Traverse 28. It fit just above the back of my neck and I found it uncomfortable, plus the narrow frame made it difficult to distribute my gear. There just wasn't enough room for everything I had planned to take. I settled on an Osprey Manta 36 Hydration Pack.

Another fortunate moment came when Sportsmart announced it was going out of business. It was a sudden move, no warning at all. The clearance sale started the day following the announcement, and I didn't hesitate to capitalize on the decision to close its doors since the timing was perfect.

I showed up the following day and purchased socks, earplugs, sunglasses, gloves, and sandals. Of all the Sportsmart purchases, I took everything but the sandals. I left the sandals after testing them a couple of times on hiking trails and noticed that they weren't secure enough during descents. I settled for a pair of Ecco Yucatan Sandals from REI. Best decision ever! I loved the Ecco sandals, and I still do. The Sportsmart purchases were non-refundable, so I spent time at the store carefully selecting items I needed and was pretty sure I would take to Spain. I was well on my way. When all was said and done, my gear consisted of the following items...

- *Osprey 36 Hydration Pack*
- *2 pairs of Lightweight Wool Hiking Socks*
- *2 pairs of footies*
- *Merrel Moab Waterproof Hiking Shoes*
- *Ecco Hiking Boots*
- *Flip-flops*
- *Convertible hiking pants*
- *York Nordic Travel Folding Walking Poles*
- *IFLYING Multiple-use Bag (Used as a fanny pack)*
- *CAMTOA Outdoor Sleeping Bag*
- *100% Pure Mulberry Silk Single Sleeping Bag Liner*
- *Sarong – cut in half and used as a towel*
- *Bandana to double as a hand towel*
- *Mini IPAD*
- *iPod / headphones*
- *Samsung cell phone*
- *2 quick dry tee shirts*
- *1 quick dry long sleeve shirt*
- *2 quick dry tank tops*
- *1 pair long leggings*
- *1 pair short leggings*
- *2 sport bras*
- *Light windbreaker*
- *Rain jacket*

- *Cap/Headband*
- *Knee Brace*
- *Nail Clippers & File*
- *Mini Flashlight*
- *90-800mg Ibuprofen/Acetaminophen with codeine for extreme knee pain*
- *Compede*
- *Bathtub stopper*
- *Toothbrush and toothpaste*
- *Deodorant*
- *2 mini bars of soap*
- *4-Port European Wall USB Charger*
- *Small Canon Camera*

I debated taking my Mini IPAD and iPod. I love to read, and I love music. I imaged walking long days listening to the wide array of music on my iPod, and then retreating to some secluded area of an albergue or hotel after a shower and dinner to journal or read from the collection of books on my Mini iPad. My daughter thought I was insane. She questioned – relentlessly I might add – why I was taking an IPAD and iPod at all when I could easily put books and music on my cell phone. Sound simple. I heard what she had to say, and with reasonable seriousness considered taking only my cell phone. I ended up taking all three. My rational was safety. I wanted my cell phone for emergency use only. What if I was strained somewhere? My cell phone would be a way of being found. (I had promised my daughter I would keep my location on at all times). I needed the cell phone battery to last from one location to the next.

Over the next couple of months, I began organizing my gear, trying my best to purchase and take only what was necessary. Like most other pilgrims, I was conscious of achieving a desired weight – 10% of my body weight – for my backpack and its contents. But that was a problem.

For the most part, my normal weight fell between 155-160 lbs. (70–72 kg). The goal was to lose about 10lbs (4.5 kg) by the time I left for Spain. I had four months to do it, and I was active, walking and hiking regularly, and burning up miles. My eating, on the other hand, was becoming something of a problem.

Everyday I have a routine: awake around 5:30am, feed my dog, fix my breakfast and lunch, walk Peter, come back and prepare for work. Breakfast was usually a fruit and spinach smoothie, or Canadian bacon, an egg, and herbal tea. For lunch, a salad with grilled chicken and other healthy items like cucumber, bean sprouts, yellow or orange peppers, and a light dressing. Most days, dinner was two chicken tacos, broiled fish and vegetables, or popcorn and wine for those times I didn't feel like cooking or dirtying my kitchen. There were times when I wouldn't eat dinner at all. Instead, against my better judgment, I would stop before getting home and grab a candy bar or some chips. This didn't help the desire to lose weight. The more I strayed away from my semi-clean eating habits, the more weight I started to gain. On May 31st, the day I left for Spain, I had gained 8lbs (4kgs). That would have allowed my backpack to weigh 16lbs (7kgs), but that weight was not a good idea for me.

Nine years ago, I made an appointment to see an orthopedic doctor about the pain and swelling in my right knee. The first doctor I visited took x-rays and diagnosed the problem as a torn meniscus. I was relieved since a torn meniscus was repairable. The doctor called in his assistance and told her to set me up with a date for surgery. Just like that. Sound simple and nothing about it seemed too serious. I left the office feeling relieved, yet a little skeptical.

Something about the quick decision to have surgery didn't sit well with me. After two days of uncertainty, I asked a coach friend for his opinion, and he confirmed what I had been thinking; get a second opinion. He gave me the number of a well-respected orthopedic doctor, located conveniently near my home, and after my visit and extensive x-rays, the good doctor broke the news that I had arthritis. I knew very little about arthritis, other than it came with soreness and swelling. Stunned, I asked the only question I could think of. *Can it be fixed?* His matter-of-fact response was, *No. You have to learn to live with it.* He advised me to get lean and stay lean. Deep down, I knew he was right; I needed to lose weight.

I had gained close to 20lbs (9kg) during the past ten years. The added weight only exacerbated the arthritis. It was my biggest concern about walking the Camino. In May, several weeks before I left for the Camino, I visited the good doctor again for my yearly Platelet Rich Plasma (PRP) injection. This would be my third year. I still lived with pain in my right knee, but with the injection, I never had to give up walking, hiking, biking or going to the gym. The benefit of the injection was the recovery time. I could do all the physical activities I loved doing – with the exception of running – and the pain during and after was always bearable, and I could sleep at night without having to take medication or elevating my knee. With the good doctor's blessing, prescriptions, and insistence that I take a good knee brace and hiking poles, I left his office assured I could complete the 500-mile journey. I had decided to give myself 36 days to complete the Camino. It seemed reasonable.

Peter would stay in a doggie daycare/hotel, and thankfully, the cost wasn't as expensive as I thought it would be. My mail had been put on hold. My neighbor and friend would check on my house while I was away.

Since I was leaving work two weeks before the end of the school year, my students' grades had been posted, and my substitute had accepted the job.

I had my euros, the bank and credit card companies were notified of my travel plans. My cell phone plan was adjusted to allow me to text and email my family and use social media to stay in contact with the people who would be concerned about me. I was ready. At least I hoped I was ready.

The day of my departure, everything on my to-do list had been taken care of, but I was a mess. I hadn't slept much; I was anxious and scared. My stomach was in knots, and I couldn't eat. I played my dream scenario over and over in my head; I would defy the odds and escape extreme pain, blisters, and I would never get lost. In a perfect world, I would meet amazing, friendly, willing-to-help people from all over the world. I would laugh and rarely be alone, and when I was, it would be by choice.

In the back of mind, the reality was that the world was not perfect and shit happens. I just wanted to be able to handle whatever came my way.

Just before time to leave home, I decided to remove a few items from my 14lbs (6kgs) backpack. I removed detergent packets I had bought at the last minute, a sweater, and an extended battery pack. I left home with my pack weighing 12.5lbs (5kgs).

I arrived at the Los Angeles International Airport three hours before departure. To preserve my knee, I checked my backpack and poles. I was prepared for the five-hour flight to JFK Airport in New York.

I am used to traveling alone; I've done it all my adult life. This trip, however, would be different because I had never traveled overseas alone, I would arrive in a part of Europe I had never been before, and I would be there for 36 days. I spoke very little Spanish – mostly words and phrases, and I worried about surviving for 36 days on what I knew.

I had a 3½-hour layover at JFK. I loved New York and for a moment, wished I could go out and explore the city, if only for a moment. I arrived at Madrid – Barajas Airport early the following morning, picked up my backpack from baggage claim and got my passport stamped. Outside, I grabbed a taxi that took me to Madrid Atocha Train Station. This moment was a lesson as the taxi driver charged me 30 euros for a ride that was less than 15 minutes. I knew I had been taken advantage of when he didn't use the meter.

Traveling solo has a way of heightening one's senses. It is like a sixth sense is awaken, something that comes to life when there's the potential of danger or being put in a stressful situation. I grew up in a tough area of Chicago and back then, I didn't know it was tough. It was my home, but I learned early on about surviving the city's sometimes-mean streets.

The taxi ride wasn't a situation of danger, but I knew charging so much for such a short distance was exploiting my language limitation and me being a tourist. Nevertheless, I paid the 30-euro fee and decided not to let the situation get the best of me. I would be in this country for more than a month, and to make the best of my visit, I needed to get a grip, be smarter about riding taxis, and keep it moving.

The 3-hour train ride from Madrid to Pamplona was beautiful and relaxing after 10 hours of flying. I enjoyed the scenery of the beautiful countryside and my conversations with the porter and a gentleman headed to Pamplona for a few days. Once in Pamplona, I watched as other backpack-carrying pilgrims exited the station. I knew that I needed to take a taxi to St. Jean de Pied Port, France, so I followed five people with backpacks as they exited the train station. They walked to a waiting vehicle that appeared to have been reserved for them. I stood for a moment, looked around, and that's when I saw a young Black woman carrying a backpack.

I knew there would be diversity on the Camino, at least I hoped there would be, but I didn't expect to meet another African American woman. Since she was wearing a backpack, I decided to approach her and make conversation, and couldn't believe my luck. Coleen was from the East Coast and had recently moved to New Mexico. This was one of those moments when I believed the forces were working in my favor. Coleen, myself and another couple from Brazil split the cost of a taxi from Pamplona to SJPdP, France, our starting point of the 500-mile (800km) Camino de Santiago. We each spent 25 euros for the beautiful 46-mile (74km) ride over the Pyrenees Mountains to SJPdP.

The taxi ride was the pilgrim-bonding moment for each of us. We were staying in separate hotels, but we liked one another immediately and decided to meet later and have dinner together. Coleen and I were both hitting the Camino trail the following morning, while the Brazilian couple was staying in SJPdP an extra day.

Once we arrived, I left my group and checked into the Hotel Itzalpea, operated by a French woman and her daughter. About eight years ago, I had visited Paris for the second time in my life, and this small and efficient hotel reminded me of a typical size European hotel. In America, oversized hotel rooms with space and amenities are expected and preferred. European hotels are more compact with fewer creature comforts. I was more than happy with the accommodations.

After a couple hours of rest, I went out to explore the charming town. With a population of about 1800 people, SJPdP had a postcard feel. It was surrounded by the Pyrenees Mountains and had a beautiful water stream running through it. I thought for a moment about staying for an additional day, just to enjoy the town's beauty, but I was anxious about the trail and prolonging my departure wasn't the answer. I needed to get started.

Coleen and I met at the pilgrims office where each of us picked up a trail map and gave a donation for the customary shell to attach to our backpack. Wearing the shell identifies pilgrims as they walk the Camino.

The narrow cobblestone street where the pilgrims office was located had restaurants and pilgrim shops. Coleen and I walked from one end of the street to the next exploring the quaint shops and boutiques.

That evening, Coleen, Bob and Gina from Brazil, and I ate at a nearby pizzeria. The place served a traditional pilgrims meal of chicken, potatoes, salad, dessert and all the wine you could drink, but knowing pilgrim meals would be on every menu for the next 36 days, I ate pizza and Coleen had a burger and fries. After dinner and great conversations, we all parted ways, and wished one another safe travels and *Buen Camino*. Coleen and I hoped we would cross paths with Bob and Gina again along the Camino.

PART I

The Journey Begins

St. Jean Pied de Port to Orisson

4.7 miles (7.6km)

Coleen and I had decided to eat breakfast before leaving for the trail. We both had made reservations to stay at the Orisson Albergue, a 4.7-mile (7.6km) hike up the Pyrenees from SJPdP. All the research and comments from other pilgrims recommended staying in Orisson. The best way to reserve a bed at the Orisson Albergue is by email (*refuge.orisson@wanadoo.fr*). I sent my request mid-April and happily received an approval email within three days. The next step was to pay. Once the albergue received my payment, the reservation was confirmed.

After breakfast on the morning of our departure, Coleen and I visited the pilgrims office to get our first official pilgrims stamp. The night before, Coleen and I spotted a chapel that we decided to visit before hitting the trail. We entered and both of us lit candles and prayed for the safe journeys of fellow pilgrims and for ourselves. With a few more photos and one last look back, we were on our way.

Neither of us considered taking the less strenuous Valcarlos Route out of SJPdP. We chose the Napoleon Route knowing the challenge of its steep climb into Orisson. Coleen and I agreed to leave SJPdP at 12:00pm. She and I both thought four hours would be more than enough time to make it, and our reservations at the Orisson Albergue were secure until 6:00pm.

Sure, I'd read about the initial climb out of SJPdP; some considered it the most challenging part of the Camino. Depending on the level of training, it could very well be the most difficult part of the trail. For me, with my moderate training and physical condition, it was damn challenging.

In the not-very-high mountainous terrains of Southern California, it would take about an hour and forty-five minutes to travel the same distance. This was different because I don't remember seeing any leveled ground out of SJPdP during the ascent into the Pyrenees. The switchbacks were constant, some more intense than others, and they seemed never-ending and straight up. There were moments when I was consciously thinking, *One foot in front of the other. Don't stop!* There were other times when I had to stop to catch my breath. About halfway to Orisson, the beauty of the Pyrenees and the open land made me appreciate the opportunity to be on this journey. This wasn't necessarily a religious journey for me, but I knew the journey itself would be significant and I expected it would be life-changing in some manner. I have the greatest appreciation for nature, and this moment, this location, this beauty, struck me so hard, I sat for a moment just to appreciate the beauty of it all.

I gave thanks and took pictures before resuming the trek. There were still times when I became winded and fatigued, but it wasn't an impossible hike. In fact, I was so into the beauty of the mountains that when I turned the corner of the last switchback and saw the albergue, I was surprised. I imagined if I wasn't staying at the Orisson Albergue, I might have thought differently, but the short hike wasn't that bad, particularly since I had traveled 14 hours to get to SJPdP, dealt with a 9-hour time change, and the altitude adjustment of being in the mountains. It took Coleen and me 3½ hours to reach Orisson.

I couldn't have asked for a better introduction to the albergue life than what I experienced at the Orisson Albergue. The view of the Pyrenees from the terrace across the road was breathtaking. While in SJPdP, I had seen my share of fellow pilgrims, but other than Coleen and the Brazilian couple, there had been no other interactions. This was an exciting moment, and I sensed the positive vibe of the other pilgrims.

The beauty of staying at the Orisson Albergue was the experience of our first true pilgrims meal on the trail. What a wonderful and unique experience it was. The meal consisted of squash soup, chicken legs and thighs, and green peas and potatoes. Let me just say, normally I would never eat green peas; I hated them as a child. Thankfully, my mother wasn't one to say; *You'll eat them or else.* She was satisfied that I tried, but I could never stomach them. For this meal, I ate green peas. Not that I planned to include them in any of my regular meal rotations, but I ate them. It's the Camino way.

At the Orisson Albergue, the tradition that followed the pilgrims meal was for everyone to introduce themselves and tell where they were from. These were the people you started the Camino with, expected to see often on the trails, and hoped to meet up with in Santiago. You would know them by name, and they would remain in your thoughts and prayers throughout the journey. Some of them may become your friends.

That night, I met people from many other parts of the world. Canada, South Africa, Denmark, Puerto Rico, and Asia. One couple was from my home state, California. The husband was walking half the distance with his wife, then he would return home, and their daughter would arrive and finish the journey with her mother.

A French man was walking his fifth Camino. He wasn't sure about returning for a sixth year. His story was fascinating. He'd had a heart attack that he thought was due to his very stressful job. As soon as he was able, he decided to walk the Camino as a way to find and maintain mental and physical balance. He looked like a man at peace, and he appeared to be in great physical condition. Two women from South Africa planned to walk for two weeks and return the following year to walk two more weeks. They hoped to complete the journey to Santiago in four years.

After dinner and wine, great conversations with interesting people, and ordering a sandwich for the next day's journey, it was time for bed. I don't think any of us had a problem sleeping. I know I didn't.

My first night in an albergue was pleasant. I shared a room that slept six with Coleen, a husband and wife from Japan, and the two women from South Africa.

**** *Albergue Orisson* – *a must if you can stay, great staff, incredible view of the Pyrenees, first official pilgrims meal on the Camino*

Orisson to Roncesvalles

8 miles (17km)

This was not a day I looked forward to. There was still more climbing to do and more switchbacks. There were still many more hours to go before my feet would be on leveled ground again. The Pyrenees was turning out to be quite an opening act in the Camino saga.

The day began with moderate fog, an overcast sky, and my body aching like crazy. My feet, knee, and thighs were sore, and my back was stiff, so I decided to get something to drink and eat then take ibuprofen that I hoped would get me through the day.

Of course, there was the doubt. It was never far away, and it took all I had to beat down the uncertainty of whether or not I could finish this journey. I had to work hard to concentrate on the task at hand, which was getting out of the Pyrenees. There was nothing I could compare this moment to. Nothing. I was in a foreign country, embarking on a 500-mile journey. I had no point of reference.

The climb out of Orisson began almost immediately. At one point, the morning fog lifted and the sun came out to expose the extraordinary views of the Pyrenees, endless skies, and herds of sheep that somehow managed to graze and run up and down steep mountainsides. There were beautiful blond-maned horses, grazing without concern of passing pilgrims. It was fantastic. I read somewhere that the Pyrenees are thought to be the most beautiful part of the Camino de Santiago. I would have to agree.

The switchbacks were less steep than yesterday; they were longer, occupied by grazing horses and sheep. There were shepherds tending to their flocks and a taxi patrolling the road, availing itself, I guessed, to weary pilgrims.

I knew this was an 8-mile trek and that it wouldn't be easy. After about four hours, I was tired and winded. My 800m Ibuprofen had kicked in, so there was no knee or feet pain. There were moments when I was so fatigued, and moments when I would count steps to see how many I could do before I was forced to stop and catch my breath. Sometimes I could push hard and do as many as 100 steps. Others times, 20 steps before stopping was all I could manage.

Along the way, I met Al, a young man from South Carolina who was hiking part of the Camino to support his two aunts. He was charismatic, with a million dollar smile. As we talked, I was trying to think of one young male member of my family who would willingly accompany me on my Camino pilgrimage. I never asked any of them, but I couldn't think of one who would put his youthful, urban lifestyle on hold to do this. Plus, not to undermine any of the young men I knew personally, the Camino isn't for everyone. Al seemed genuinely excited to be there.

Seeing pictures of landmarks along The Way, as the Camino is sometimes called, made my adventure seemed more real. I appreciated seeing the statue of the Virgin Vierge d'Orisson Vierge de Biakorri. The statue seemed to be a popular stopping spot for pilgrims who boldly climbed the rocks to get a closer view and capture priceless photos of the statue and its surroundings of rolling mountains and valleys.

The landmark Cruceiro, a short hike ahead, indicated a change in the route that veered to the right of the main road. The France/Spain border was just ahead. The summit was breathtaking. Although I was anxious to get this leg of my journey over with, I couldn't help but stop and take in the view and appreciate my short-term accomplishment. I also had to consider the dilemma ahead; there were two routes out of the Pyrenees. One route was known to be dangerous and has caused injuries, even ended the pilgrimage for some. By this time, I was tired, and my knee had started to hurt. Instead of the risky route, I opted for the alternative road that I knew would be less taxing on my knee, but would add time to my descent.

The alternative road wasn't difficult, but it was long. There was a time, after not seeing another person, that I thought I had missed a turn-off somewhere. It was a while before I saw the only other two people on the road out of the mountain. The road then led to a brief stretch of highway before the entrance into Roncesvalles.

When I was preparing for this journey, I didn't believe for one minute that I could do it without periods of some pain. In fact, I expected that my trip over the Pyrenees would be one of those moments. It was the start of a long journey, and I knew pain would be a part of the adjustment. So while making reservations for rooms in SJPdP and Orisson, I reserved rooms at hotels in Roncesvalles and Pamplona. I thought it would be necessary to assess my body and the degree of pain during the first week of my Camino.

In the beautiful medieval town of Roncesvalles, I stayed at the Hotel Roncesvalles. After checking in and taking a much-needed shower, I later joined Coleen at the Iglesia de Santa Maria Cathedral for mass, where pilgrims from all faiths are welcome to receive blessings for a safe journey. It was a beautiful and touching ceremony.

Reaching Roncesvalles was a milestone for me. I felt as if the Pyrenees were an initiation that I had gotten through successfully, and now I could move forward and settle into the journey of walking the Camino de Santiago.

After dinner, the pilgrims mass, a little sightseeing, and another nice long shower, I was ready for bed. The fatigue of two days and 14 miles in the Pyrenees, jetlag from ten hours of flying and the 9-hour time different had caught up with me. I was exhausted, but I felt good that I had made it over the Pyrenees.

***** **Roncesvalles** – *great, medieval town, small with some shops, wonderful cathedral – the pilgrims mass a must*

***** **Hotel Roncesvalles** – *great location, nice clean, modern room, great restaurant with good food.*

Roncesvalles to Zubiri

13.6 miles (21.9km)

The Pyrenees was my initiation into the Camino. The mountains were intense, and I looked forward to a milder terrain where I wouldn't be so fatigued and winded as I walked. To me, Roncesvalles seemed like the true official start of my Camino. Maybe it was all the pilgrims gathered at the Iglesia de Santa Maria Cathedral for the pilgrims mass, or it could have been the breathtaking medieval town itself.

I was sore. My calves and right knee hurt. I started my day with what would become my favorite Camino breakfast: a croissant, fresh squeezed orange juice and a café leche (coffee with milk), and an 800mg ibuprofen (sometimes a half, sometimes a whole one). At home, herbal tea is my morning beverage of choice, but I found the stimulation of caffeine welcoming at the start of each day on the Camino. I'm also not a big bread eater, but the thought that I could have all the bread I wanted and not have it affect my weight – because of the mileage I would put in daily – was reason enough to eat it everyday, sometimes three times a day. For the next 36 days, I decided that I wouldn't restrict my food choices. If I saw it and I wanted it, I would eat it.

At the start of the trail out of Roncesvalles, I stood in a short line and took pictures for a few pilgrims while I patiently waited to have my photo taken in front of the landmark sign, Santiago 790km. It seemed almost impossible at the time, and because of the way my body was feeling, I wondered if it would ever adjust to the demands of walking great distances everyday to make it to Santiago.

For the second day, Coleen and I started out on the trail together, but, like yesterday, we soon parted ways. I was 61 and a mere 5ft, 5in, and she in her thirties and a long-legged 5ft 10in. She and I had determined our next destination over breakfast. This became a system. We would eat breakfast together and discuss the weather, and the estimated time it would take to arrive at the next location. She always arrived at the destination before me; a good thing, I might add. Although she wasn't allowed to register me – the person staying had to show their passport to register – she could get the person running the place to hold my bed until my arrival. There is a saying on the Camino, *The Camino provides.* I knew from the moment I met Coleen at the train station that she was my Camino angel. Because of what I'd read from other pilgrim experiences, one of my biggest fears on the Camino was that I would arrive at an albergue and no rooms would be available. With Coleen, I didn't have that fear.

After taking photos in Roncesvalles, Colleen and I were both excited to begin our journey to Zubiri. This leg of the journey was different from the Pyrenees. The trail passed through wooded areas, rolling valleys of quaint little towns and villages, with beautifully flower-decorated homes surrounded by mountains. I didn't pay much attention to cars in SJPdP, but here there were Volvos, Mercedes Benz, and Peugeots. There was, surprisingly, a small Ford tractor in one of the towns. This was also where I started my appreciation of the sounds and beauty of the many crystal clear rivers I would see on the Camino. I was a slow walker and I often found myself alone. It wasn't a bad thing since there were always people just ahead of me.

Because I had researched so much about the Camino, I was familiar with the landmarks and often-photographed spots. After stopping for lunch at a café, I was surprised to walk up on the stop sign that had been graffiti'd to read 'Don't Stop Walking.' The sign was on the cover of one of the first books I read about the Camino.

Another beauty of the Camino was the convenience of cafes along the trails that catered to pilgrims. Each day's journey was thankfully broken up by short stops that allowed hikers to rest and enjoy local foods and beverages. During one stop at a cafe in Viskerreta, I sat with Julia from the Netherlands. She and a few others were tending to feet problems. Julia had a small bag filled with supplies for her feet. This was her second time doing the Camino, and she said the experience of the first taught her that more than Compede was necessary. Her feet had taken a beating during her first Camino, and the biggest lesson she came away with was the importance of foot care *before* things got too serious. She sat at the table with a sandwich and a beer taping her toes and heels. She spoke of having a new 'hot spot' – that warm, tingling, uncomfortable feeling that occurs when a blister is about to form.

I asked what all did she had in her bag. The last time she walked the Camino, which was three years prior, she was off her feet for three days because of blisters. This year, she came prepared. She brought three rolls of tape, cotton balls, needle and thread, a set of cuticle clippers, a small bottle of mercuricome, and alcohol wipes. I felt unprepared. The only foot care products I brought were a small nail clipper to keep my toenails short and Compede, something Julia didn't have. She had tried Compede during her last Camino and didn't like it.

Since this adventurous vacation thing was new to me and my feet, I hadn't known what to expect. I'd read that some people walk the entire Camino without getting a single blister. Others had foot problems ranging from blisters to the loss of toenails, and everything in between. I hadn't experienced any pain that made me think I needed taping or Compede yet, but I was concerned about not being ready for unexpected blisters. I decided then that as soon as I found a pharmacy, I would buy the necessary supplies for my feet, just in case.

The rest of the day's journey was tiring, not too bad until the descent into Zubiri. By that time, I had started to compile quite a few photos. I was using my cell phone exclusively (I also had a small Canon camera that I never used). My practically new cell phone was doing a great job. I was overwhelmed by the beauty and experience of the Camino and had decided to take as many memorable photos as I possibly could.

As much as I had wanted to take pictures of the last mile before Zubiri, I couldn't. I wouldn't dare. The descent out of the Pyrenees paled in comparison to this descent. I was actually amazed that I made it down the path paved with jagged rocks without falling and hurting myself. It was intense and scary. There was no stopping and some people, those who seemed more experienced and comfortable with this area, were breezing down with little or no effort. Most were handling the descent with hiking poles, some without. I couldn't imagine it without my poles. In fact, it was right after this descent that Coleen decided to get poles. She was lucky that some kind soul gave her one of their poles while descending into Zubiri, and as soon as she found a store that sold pilgrim gear, she bought another.

There were some people (like me) descending into Zubiri using the switchback method: a kind of a one-side-of-the-trail-to-the-other form of walking that is supposed to be easier on knees. I had to take it slow, super slow, and be conscious of every step I took.

At one point, three women behind me were closing in on me and obviously wanted to pass. It wasn't an issue, but the women attempted to do it while walking side by side and the trail wasn't that wide. The ladies were making me nervous, so I hugged one side of the trail and allowed them to pass. For some reason, I couldn't imagine why, they stopped in the middle of the trail, right in front of me. They spoke French, and I clearly hoped they would understand my words and my direct tone when I said, *Please move.* They parted, and I moved passed them. For the rest of the descent, they stayed behind me.

Something I've known for most of my adult life was reaffirmed on the Camino. *Keep everything in prospective.* It became my mantra on the Camino. The Camino was proving to be a challenge that was more mental than physical. It was presenting me with an ebb and flow of emotions, and pain, and people. The descent into Zubiri was taking its toll.

Since I first learned I had arthritis in my right knee; I had adjusted my physical activities with the intent of keeping the arthritis from getting worse, to avoid surgery for as long as I could. I once loved wearing five-inch heels, but I no longer wore them. I no longer ran, something I also enjoyed. In the past, it had been nothing for me to enter local a 10k or half marathon, sometimes doing as many as thirty a year. Before my arthritis diagnosis, I was working my way up to doing a marathon.

I always thought I had a strong tolerance for pain, so I didn't totally rule out continuing my running regiment or working toward my marathon ambition after finding out about the arthritis, not until the good doctor informed me that running was out. So I accepted doing 10ks or half marathons. Doing a marathon – like climbing Mt. Everest – became just a dream.

Over the course of time, I had discovered what agitated my knee the most. The local mountains and hills I frequented in Southern California soon helped me conclude that steep descents were my biggest agitation. No descent, however, had prepared me for this descent into Zubiri.

When I finally arrived in Zubiri, saying I was relieved would be an understatement. Zubiri was an oasis. As I crossed the bridge into the town, I saw a fair number of pilgrims soaking their feet in the beautiful running stream of water outside of the albergue where I would be staying. I planned to join them as soon as I had showered and eaten.

The Albergue Zaldiko welcomed weary pilgrims with open arms. This was the albergue Coleen and I had decided on the previous night during dinner. It was after 3:00pm when I arrived, and all the beds had been reserved. I couldn't begin to express how grateful I was to have Coleen. By securing a bed for me upon her arrival, I didn't have to search other albergues in Zubiri that were probably completely booked as well. *The Camino provides.* If that had happened, my only choice would have been to continue on to the next town of Larrasoaña, another 3 miles (5.6k) beyond Zubiri.

Wouldn't you know it? I had a blister, a small one, but a blister, nonetheless. It was my first blister ever. Earlier on the trail to Zubiri, I was starting to feel that warm, tingly sensation on the side of my big toe, but I was sure I had enough time to get to the albergue and treat it before it manifested into something ugly.

I asked the lady who ran the albergue if she had a needle and thread. She did, but instead of giving it to me, she instructed me to sit. She spoke English quite well and gave me a lesson on draining my blister using the needle and thread method. She did the procedure for me, for which I was grateful. With the thread securely laced through where the rising on the left side of my big toe, I was ready to go out and tour Zubiri.

My first stop was to soak my aching feet in the river stream; it was heaven. The ice-cold water provided instant relief to my sore feet. About an hour later, I was able to walk to the restaurant where Coleen and I had agreed to meet. She and I sat outside the café and enjoyed a pilgrims meal of chicken, potatoes, salad, and wine. Kathy from Montreal, Canada soon joined us. I remember seeing her at the Albergue Orisson but hadn't had the chance to meet or speak to her. Like Coleen and me, Kathy was also traveling solo. Her husband and adult children were supportive of her dream to walk the Camino. The three of us enjoyed our meal and shared stories of our respective lives back home and our Camino experience so far. We all looked forward to relaxing in Pamplona. Coleen and I were staying an extra night in Pamplona. Kathy would be there for one night.

All my pains resurfaced during the short walk back to the albergue. I had no energy left to tour the town or check out the few shops that had clothing and other gear for pilgrims. I was hurting so I went back to the albergue, climbed into the top bunk I had been assigned and slept. But the sleep won't last.

Sometime during the night, my knee started to ache. Normally, if I experienced extreme knee pain at home, I would elevate my knee using several pillows and combat the pain with two or three over-the-counter ibuprofen. I had only one pillow here, and my bunk wasn't near a wall for me to rest my knee against. I did the best I could with the one pillow, but the throbbing pain was intense, and my knee was swollen. I had two kinds of pain pills prescribed by my orthopedic doctor, and I decided to take the stronger one. It helped with the pain, but not the swelling. Before I drifted off to sleep, I made the decision to take the bus to Pamplona. Not an easy decision, especially so early in my journey. I hoped that a day off the trail and two nights in Pamplona would give me time to heal and keep my journey from ending so soon.

***** *Zubiri* – *great town, a pilgrim shop, great restaurant area*

***** *Albergue Zuldiko* – *a must for anyone staying in Zubiri, great hospitality – the nice lady did my laundry for a small fee, and the nearby river stream was wonderful.*

Zubiri to Pamplona. (Sad face)

13 miles (20.9km)

The following morning, Coleen, who also had a blister, but wasn't having joint problems, left for the 13-mile (20.9k) hike to Pamplona. Feeling better because of the medication, but sore just the same, I walked about two miles to the bus stop and waited for the bus to Pamplona. As I walked, I passed an elementary school that was about to begin its day. The wait for the bus was about an hour. I sat with Sophia, from Italy. She was a pretty, thin young lady with a large, oversized backpack. She and I talked about our adventures on the Camino and our disappointment with having to take the bus. Her backpack, she told me, was filled with medication. She was a diabetic, and suffered from a rare blood disorder. Sophia was one of a few brave souls I met on the Camino with medical issues that required carrying addition weight of must-have medications. Talking with Sophia and hearing her declaration to complete the Camino, even if she had to return several more times to get it done, made my knee problem seem like a small burden. If this courageous young lady with life-threating medical issue could remain so positive, who the hell was I to complain about an achy knee?

After getting dropped off at a bus stop in Pamplona, Sophia and I hugged, said our goodbyes, and extended well wishes to each other. I left her at the bus stop in Pamplona with a new profound determination to live up to the challenge of making it to Santiago. From time to time, I wondered about Sophia while I was on the Camino, but I never saw her again.

Finding my hotel was the next task at hand. Hotel Tres Reyes was the hotel I had reserved before leaving California. I first had to find its location, which, I soon discovered, was on the opposite side of Pamplona from where the bus had dropped me off.

Pamplona was fascinating. It was the one city that I knew something about. I had no real knowledge of St. Jean Pied de Port or Roncesvalles. Pamplona is home to The Running of the Bulls. That I knew. The city is known for its many festivals and family-oriented culture, and joyful atmosphere.

There was a book fair going on in Pamplona's city center when I arrived. It was still morning, and I couldn't register in the hotel until 3:00pm, so I stopped at one of the nearby cafes for a bite to eat and decided to sit outside and watch the people of Pamplona.

Pamplona was the first large city on the Camino. It was beautiful, busy, and just the right size to get around on foot.

Walking from the opposite side of the city to where my hotel was located was not too bad, sore knee and feet considered. There were many cafes, clothing and novelty shops and, thankfully, pharmacies. I stopped at the first one I saw; everything there was out in the open, unlike in America where doctor-prescribed medication is behind a counter and accessible only to pharmacist and technicians. The pharmacist here was available to speak with directly if needed. She was gracious in answering my questions about foot care. She recommended a cream for keeping my feet soft and moisturized, tape and cotton balls, needle and thread, small scissors and mecuricome for cleaning and preventing infection. I also purchased ibuprofen cream for my knee, along with the recommended foot care items. I didn't need the extra weight in my backpack while on the trail, but I made a mental note to purchase extra tubes of the knee cream in Santiago to take home with me.

Clear on the other side of Pamplona was the Hotel Tres Reyes. I wasn't sure how far I walked, but it was quite a distance; about two miles, I imagined. The Hotel Tres Reyes was the largest hotel I stayed in during my Camino. Coleen was still on the trail, and I knew she wouldn't arrive until 3:00pm or later. It was a perfect time to check in and relax for a while. The registration clerk was very accommodating. My knee was on fire, and he kindly provided me with an ice pack and recommended that I take advantage of the hotel's masseuse.

It was nice to be off my feet and rest my knee. I welcomed the 3-hour nap and had to fight the strong urge to go out and further explore Pamplona. The lone time gave me the opportunity to think seriously about my knee pain. The ice helped with the pain, but the swelling and stiffest persisted. As much as I regretted being off the trail, I knew taking the bus was the right thing to do.

Another option would have been to stay an extra day or two in Zubiri and not miss the trail to Pomplona. It was one of those things that I started to beat myself up about. Had I failed the Camino already? Was I meant to do this or not? I questioned myself and began to seriously overthink my decision to take the bus to Pamplona. I hadn't found my *groove* on the Camino and wondered if I ever would.

Coleen arrived around 4:00pm. Once she had showered, changed and rested, we ventured down to the hotel restaurant for food. This leg of the journey had been a struggle for her as well. She was sore and now had two blisters, and since we both were staying an extra day, we agreed to eat in the hotel and spend the day resting. We would explore Pamplona the following day.

It had taken only four days to realize there were tell-tell signs to recognizing pilgrims: oversized backpacks for one, and of course, the penguin walk – the walk of soreness and fatigue. It was something to think about. Each day of the pilgrimage required every person, no matter how they felt, to rise early each morning, re-pack and re-adjust backpacks, and engage in proper foot care to carry you to the next location, while ignoring pain and sometimes injury.

DAY 5

Pamplona
Rest day

After a good night's sleep and a leisure morning of me checking emails and Facebook-ing family and friends, and Coleen Facetime-ing her children, we felt good enough to go out and explore Pamplona. Plus, we were hungry. The morning sun was bright, and the air was warm. Coleen and I were clean and happy to be able to wear sandals instead of hiking shoes. It felt so good to walk without a backpack, although I quietly longed for the aide of my hiking poles. We carried fanny packs, wore casual shorts, tee shirts and caps, and looked very much like the touristy pilgrims we were. We laughed hard at the way the other walked. She and I decided that after eating breakfast, we would find the masseuse recommended by the hotel clerk. I wasn't necessarily restricted to a hard-lined budget, so getting a massage at a fairly reasonable cost was a priority.

We walked through the popular area of Pamplona where we saw a massage parlor. We dashed in hoping to get an immediate appointment, but sadly we had to turn around and leave when told they were booked for the day.

Pamplona turned out to be the perfect place to take a break from the Camino. It is a moderately small city of about a quarter of a million people. It had a homey, small-town feel to it, perfect for walking around and enjoying the sights. There were more than enough intimate cafes and eateries to accommodate the bustling traffic of pedestrians. I have always loved the small mom-and-pop businesses of Europe. Unlike the U.S., there were no oversized grocery chains here. Instead, there were only small stores that offered limited quantities of produce and other items. Coleen and I moved at the pace of snails, but with frequent breaks for breakfast, coffee, or just sitting to people-watch, walking around the city wasn't too bad on our sore bodies.

After about two hours of touring Pamplona, we returned to the hotel for a quick rest. Before going up to our room, we found the hotel masseuse and made reservations for early-afternoon massages. Neither of us felt that full body massages were necessary, so we each opted for a 30-minute lower body massage.

Seeing a doctor couldn't have been more helpful. Dirk was from Sweden, and he had a touch that was like magic. It did the trick. When he was done, Coleen and I both were more relaxed, less sore, and felt absolutely giddy from the relief of pain and stiffness. For the remainder of my Camino pilgrimage, I followed Dirk's advice to elevate my legs for at least 30 minutes at the end of each day's hike.

That evening, Coleen and I went out to further explore Pamplona. We took our time checking out local shops while enjoying the festive atmosphere of Pamplona. The center was bustling with residents, tourist, and pilgrims. Whether or not pilgrims carried backpacks, wore sandals or hiking boots, it was pretty easy to tell who were pilgrims and who weren't. There was, of course, the walk; we all walked gingerly as if timing each step, making sure to step precisely to prevent further pain or injury. Then, there were the clothes, which were often clean, but un-pressed. And the hair was also just there; washed and brushed or pulled up in the best presentable style possible. While doing the Camino, hair is the least of most pilgrims' worry. My hair was short, and the simple process of wash it and go, worked for me. It also meant fewer items in my backpack since I didn't have a need for anything more than a comb, brush and conditioner.

As Coleen and I walked around Pamplona, we saw a few familiar faces. There were a few hellos and well wishes that were common among pilgrims. We recognized people we'd seen on the trail but had shared only a nodded greetings or a *Buen Camino.* It was a beautiful warm day, perfect for people watching. We stopped several time, just to sit outside with a glass of wine, water, a few tapas, and watch people enjoy Pamplona. As the afternoon turned into evening more and more people were out and about, enjoying the later part of the day.

It was late evening and we were ready for dinner. Coleen asked if I had a preference for food, but I did not. We agreed to walk, and with tapas and other foods in plain view of cafes, we decided to stop when and where the mood hit us. We settled on great café that was filled with people who appeared to be locals. Everyone was comfortable, talkative, and many seemed to know one another. There were children who sat as their parents and grandparents casually shared wine or beer with other locals. I found it beautiful and intimate, and I was totally impressed with this culture that embraced food and family with ease. No one was in a hurry to move on from this moment of enjoying precious family time. It was something I came to cherish while in Spain. Family time mattered most to the people of Spain. It was a priority.

It all starts, I think, with the affordable prices of food and beverages. A glass of wine in a United States bar or café would cost around $4.00 (3.30 euros) or more. In Spain, I never paid more than two euros for a glass of wine, regardless of the region, café, or albergue. Food was equally affordable. It added to the beauty of the Camino and I was grateful for that. Neither the cost of food, wine, albergue, nor occasional hotel spurge would break the bank. I realized that the Camino could be done on a very limited budget, and it appeared that local patrons could eat out and enjoy the beauty of their small cities, towns, and villages for probably little more than what it would cost to prepare a home-cooked meal. As much as I came to enjoy sharing a pilgrims meal with fellow pilgrims, I loved having food and wine in the cafés. I vowed that I would occasionally eat with fellow hikers, but decided that – whenever I could – I would explore the small cities and towns and villages of the Camino, and eat with the locals.

The evening in Pamplona ended with a festival parade through the center square that was packed with people. Flags were raised, chants and songs were heard, and my immediate thought was it was a religious celebration. Coleen and I asked someone and were told it was just a local custom to end a Friday evening with a march through the square. Whatever the reason, it was beautiful and the perfect way for Coleen and I to end our stay in Pamplona.

***** *Pamplona* – *one of my Camino favorites, so happy Coleen agreed to stay the extra day with me, I highly recommend staying in Pamplona.*

**** *Hotel Tres Reyes* – *a splurge, but well worth it, a bit far from the center square, but I loved the room and its view, and the very helpful staff.*

Pamplona to (Obanos) Puenta La Reina

15 miles (24km)

Coleen and I awoke around 6:30am and started what came to be our morning ritual of preparing for the day's hike to the next decided location. We carefully oiled our bruised and blistered feet, wrapped and taped infected areas, and other areas of our feet to keep potential blisters at bay.

The extra night in Pamplona added to the anticipation as well as the anxiety of my Camino journey. I began the day's journey by doing what I did best; I started to overthink how taking an extra day – even though it was planned and necessary – would affect my pilgrimage. I became consumed with whether or not I would make it to Santiago, or miss my planned 33-day adventure. Could I do the Camino without taking any more extra days? I was also beating myself up for taking the bus. Had I jinxed my Camino adventure by doing so?

Physically, I felt good. I headed out on the trail, and it didn't take long for Coleen to move past me to where I could no longer see her. My knee felt good and was less swollen. The overall soreness of the calves and feet had lessened, and my spirits were high.

After stopping for a café con leche, croissant, and orange juice before reaching the trail, I took half an 800m ibuprofen to eliminate the stiffness and get myself walking-ready to rejoin the other pilgrims. I didn't want to be sore, in pain, or jeopardize my adventure. I wanted to be on the trail, everyday from here to Santiago. I wanted to walk my Camino. I had missed being on the trail.

Each leg of the Camino was special, and the scenery was always different and always something to enjoy and cherish. I didn't know exactly what to expect beyond the Pyrenees, but I was never disappointed with the trail from one location to the next. Some proved to be more challenging than others, but every leg of Camino added its own unique beauty to the journey and to the unique flavor of Spain.

I quickly fell in love with the Rojas region of the Camino, the wines in particular. I love a dark, heavy body wine, and for me, wines of the Rojas region fit that bill. Also, this is where I came to appreciate the yellow jasmine bushes that sometimes lined the Camino trails. In Southern California, there is plenty of the wonderful-smelling jasmine, not as plentiful as in Spain, however.

And there were the red poppies. There were times when I'd see endless fields of red poppies, and other times when there would be fields of greenery. There were times when I would see an almost endless field of greenery and golden hay and only one poppy. It made me think about life. One poppy in a vast field of greenery. *Life always finds a way.* It was like the many times on the Camino when I'd see rocks, boulders, and dirt on trails, and all of a sudden there would be one lone poppy or some other lone flower fighting its way through, demanding its own place. It was amazing. It was moments like this that started my process deep thinking on the Camino.

As an occasional hiker, I have grown to love nature. Perhaps I've always been in love with nature, and my love for it is the very reason I started to enjoy hiking. It wasn't just for the health benefits, although I consider hiking trails the perfect gym. The sights, sound, and smells are viable reasons why so many others and I choose the outdoors over indoor gyms.

I first started hiking about seven years prior to my Camino. I'd take long walks on the walking trails of the Pacific Ocean close to where I live. Back then, and for a good long while after, I would walk for hours with headphones in my ears, and an iPod clipped to my waistband. I considered it the ultimate alone-time when I could drown out the world with music. I was never without my iPod.

Eventually, I evolved. Sometime later, I began to appreciate walking without music. The Southern California hiking trails did it for me. I started hiking with a group of co-workers, all experienced hikers. The trails we hiked were intense and unfamiliar and took all my concentration, so no iPod. At first, I cursed, and whined, and complained, and questioned why anyone would trudge through terrains that challenged both mental and physical endurance. While others hikers seemed to breeze through without so much as a whence, alone each never-ending ascent, I thought it was hellish. But the more I was exposed to the unique beauty of every trail I experienced, the more I understood and appreciated the surroundings. And I didn't have to go far to find the beauty.

The Pacific Ocean is close to my home, and each of the nearby ocean trails – my favorite kind of trail – offers its own unique sights and sounds. The sounds of the ocean, in particular, have become a great source of meditation. The beauty of plants and flowers and shrubbery, some never seen before, always give me stop-and-smell-the-roses moments. And I try to take advantage of every one of those precious moments. Odd bugs and songs of beautifully colored birds are new discoveries every single time. That is why the beauty of the Camino de Santiago appealed to me. That is why my slow, snail's pace never bothered me.

The trail to Puenta La Reina was an introduction to a new kind of beauty; it was nature at its finest. I had no idea I would be so enthralled by the simplicity of it all. I took over a hundred photos of poppies, yellow jasmine, rolling fields of greenery, trees, and picturesque homes during this leg of my Camino journey. I stopped often, not just to rest my weary body, but more so to enjoy the beauty and sounds of running rivers and small brooks. The idea to distract myself from my sore feet and muscles by listening to music wasn't going to happen...not this day.

The day's hike began relatively well. The terrain started out flat with mostly paved roads that extended from the city limits and outskirts of Pamplona. Let me just say, on the Camino, I quickly became grateful for the little, often unnoticed, unspoken things that, without a doubt, helped me along my journey. Like stopping in Orisson instead of hiking straight through to Roncesvalles, having acceptable weather conditions, the many villages and cafes, ibuprofen, pharmacies, kind people, my hiking poles, and time. All of these factors helped me ease into the job of tackling the upcoming 750m climb.

The day was pleasant—no cold, no extreme heat, and no rain. For the first time I walked in shorts, or should I say, my hiking pants with the lower leg parts zipped off. My light jacket was perfect for the cool and overcasted morning. Once the coolness of the morning broke, it would easily wrap around my waist or tuck into my backpack. I wore a lightweight tee shirt. I had seriously considered wearing my Ecco sandals and a pair of footies instead of socks, but I changed my mind just before I left the hotel. My feet felt pretty good, so with a little taping of my heels and some of my toes, I thought they would be fine.

Soon into the hike, the view of the day's challenge was just ahead. The moderate mountain was about 5 miles (8k) out of Pamplona. Seeing it evoked anticipation, unlike the nervous anxiety I felt before tackling the Pyrenees. I knew it wouldn't be the same. First, my trusty guide, *The Pilgrim's Guide to Camino de Santiago* by John Brierley indicated the difference in distance between the two. According to the guide, the peak of The Pyrenees is 4757ft (1450m), while the summit of the upcoming mountain was a *mere* 2450ft. (750m)

Coleen and I stopped at a cafe just outside Pamplona where I had my now favorite breakfast of croissant, orange juice, and cafe leche, followed by a 800m ibuprofen. We each purchased a sandwich and chips to take with us, and were soon on our way. Over dinner the previous night, she and I had agreed to stay at the Hotel Jakue, just before Puente La Reina.

Now fortified with food and medication, I began to ease into the journey of the day. Shortly after leaving the cafe, as usual, I soon lost sight of Coleen. She was an amazing hiker as were all the other younger, more fit pilgrims. I saw quite a few hikers but didn't engage in any conversation other than a few *Buen Caminos*. I saw no one I knew or had seen before. As usual, I ended up far behind the pilgrims I had seen at the start of the day.

It didn't take long to make it to the base of the day's climbing challenge. There were the familiar rocks and boulders that I soon realized, or should I say assumed – because I really didn't know for sure – were there to provide traction to pilgrims during rainy or snowy weather conditions. Without them, I imagined, heavy rains would create muddy conditions that would make it almost impossible to ascend or descend mountainous terrains. As much as I disliked walking on the rocks and boulders because they irritated my feet and exacerbated my blisters, I imagined I would feel completely different if I had to climb or descend mountains in heavy rain without the traction of rocks and boulders. I must admit, they did provide good traction during climbing, even in dry conditions.

The climb up the mountain was steep in the beginning, but became gradual after a while. Just after the initial steep ascent there was a moment on the trail where I turned around to see the incredible view of Pamplona.

The most unique and unexpected part of the climb was seeing the wind turbines that stood high on the mountain near the summit. It was strange in a sense, like watching something that you knew was there for a good reason, but it didn't seem to belong. The Camino is so historical with buildings, trails, and monuments that have been around for centuries. The ultra-modern wind turbines seemed out of place. I'm sure the benefits of having them are justifiable, but still...

Palms Springs, California is where I first saw windmills, as they are called in California. In Palms Springs, they seem endless; miles and miles of them, generating electricity for the desert regions of Southern California. I had only seen them from the comfort of a car as I drove en route to Palm Springs for a mini vacation. Here on the Camino, atop the mountain, there weren't as many, and they just seemed odd here.

The closer I got to the turbines, the more fascinated I became. They were huge, of course, but the sound... I didn't expect the turning blades to sound so powerful. I practically passed right under them and was amazed by the feel of the powerful wind caused by the enormous turning blades.

On the initial ascent, I thought there were only a few wind turbines, about 12 at the most. On the summit, just before the descent at the end of the monument, you could see the alignment of wind turbines as they snaked through the chain of mountains. There were many more than twelve.

At the summit of Alto del Perdon was the Monumento Peregrino, the first monument I looked forward to seeing. I remembered it from my research and from seeing it in the movie *The Way*. The panoramic view was equally spectacular. I walked along the monument fascinated with its structure and the honor it paid to the many pilgrims who, for many centuries, traveled this route.

At this point in my journey, I was having a love/hate, or should I say like tolerate/hate relationship with mountains and steep hills. My body reacted differently to ascents and descents, and I wondered if I'd ever find my endurance leverage. I also wondered if it would get any easier. Ascents proved easiest on my arthritic knee and also put the least amount of pressure on the blisters now forming on both heels of my feet.

I was now on the sixth day of my journey to Santiago, and although I had no idea how I should feel at this point,

I was disappointed that I was still winded with every step toward the summit of a mountain or steep hill. When climbing, I still had to step to the side of the trail to catch my breath and allow faster hikers to pass.

Summits were always my salvation; they gave me time to stop, breathe, have food, and regroup for the hike downhill. Descents were hardest on my body. While I breathed easier during downhills, my feet and my right knee took a beating every time. Descents had me praying on some days and cursing on others.

Coleen and I had agreed to stay at the Albergue Jakue, located in on the lower level of the Jakue Hotel in Obanos, a village just before Puente la Reina. When I arrived, as usual, she had already showered and washed her clothes. I was a little envious that she always finished her day on the trail an hour or so ahead of me. By the time I'd showered and taken care of my laundry, she had done the same, plus rested and Facetimed her kids back home.

I liked the albergue immediately. It had a small quaint resting area with a few tables and chairs just outside the rooms. It was a great place to sit with Coleen, catch some late afternoon sun and talk about the day's hike and how our respective bodies were holding up. Overall, Coleen was doing great, with the exception of a few blisters that didn't seem to slow her down. It wasn't a bad day's hike for me either. My feet were sore as they normally were after a long day of walking on rocks, and my developing heels blistered were irritating, but my knee was fine, which was a plus for me. She and I sat and read over our guides to review the terrain of following day's hike and determine the appropriate mileage and where we would stay. For dinner, we opted for the hotel's buffet, specially priced for pilgrims staying in the albergue.

Today's dinner was extra special; not only was the variety of food from the buffet delicious, but Coleen and I also shared our dinner table with two ladies from Germany, one from Frankfurt, the other, a neighboring small town. Sarah and Janice had been friends since high school, and though they lived about 100 miles (161k) apart, they phoned each other regularly and visited whenever time permitted.

A year prior, Sarah from Frankfurt had been feeling sick for an extended amount of time, and after an extensive round of medical tests, doctors discovered she had developed a rare form of cancer. As shallow and stereotypical as this may sound, I never would have guessed it from her physical appearance, her actions, her energy, her joy, that she was dealing with a severe illness. She had the most amazing spirit and philosophy of life. She didn't dwell on her illness, she refused to allow others around her to feel any sorrow for her, and she exuded a rare peaceful and humbling spirit that I'd seen only in a few people during my lifetime. Sarah and Janice began in Pamplona and, per doctor's orders, were only walking to Burgos, a distance of 131 miles (211k). The four of us spent several hours over numerous glasses of wines discussing life in general, and life in our respective counties. We talked about the importance of family, prioritizing, and letting go of nonessentials. We finally ended our conversation just after 8:00pm.

After dinner, Coleen and I sat in another part of the hotel and people-watched, as we liked to do. While sitting, we were joined by Uri from Finland. He was another amazing bundle of energy. He had an infectious laugh and a bubby personality. We all thought it was so funny that his wife had sent him on the 500-mile (800k) hike to lose weight. He was a crowd pleaser, and because we were laughing loudly and appeared to be having fun, we were soon joined by a few other pilgrims and hotel guests.

This was the latest I'd stayed up since I began my Camino. Pilgrims meals on the Camino usually start at 7:00pm, which was difficult for me. This night, I ended up going to bed after 10:00pm.

**** *Obanos* – *a small town on the outskirts of Puenta La Reina, nice town, close to the highway*

***** *Jakue Albergue* – *nice facility located in the basement of the Hotel Jakue, with great a food buffet, pilgrims had the option to stay at the hotel or the albergue; the albergue was perfect*

Puenta La Reina to Villatuerta

10 miles (18km)

Our day started around 6:30am. This was the first day that I paid close attention to the morning ritual of pilgrims. We all rose at similar times, some wanting to head out early enough to be on the trail when the sun rose, and some left early to get a head start on others to ensure having a room at the next desired location. Each albergue had rules and expectations about check-in time and the time for everyone to be up and out. I was a slow walker so getting up and out on the trail early was something I knew I had to do if I wanted to have a bed at our chosen location. By the time I awoke in the morning, just about every pilgrim in the albergue was also up preparing to leave.

Coleen and I rose around the same time. After taking care of restroom needs, dressing and repacking backpacks, we met up in the common seating area to begin the process of moisturizing, oiling, taping and cushioning feet to get them just right for the day's journey.

Mornings were also quiet time for pilgrims. Regardless of the developing relationships and joyous conversations had over dinner, beer and wine the previous night, mornings were solemn. And yes, last night had been a fun time and one of my more memorable evenings on the Camino. This morning, like others, there were no or very few - only necessary - words spoken as pilgrims prepared for the day's hike. Everything needed to be just right: well-balanced and properly packed backpacks, weather-ready clothing, and of course foot care. I couldn't help but watch the intensity of it all. Regardless of citizenship, age, or Camino experience, everyone did the quiet morning ritual. The longer I was on the Camino, the better I became at getting up and getting out in a timely fashion; and the better I became at doing it with minimal disturbance to others.

One of my favorite items I carried on the Camino was a small military-style flashlight given to me by a fellow teacher, a former Marine. It was a good one: compact, lightweight, with a high-powered beam that narrowed and widened by sliding the lens. It served me well for getting packed and ensuring I left nothing behind, in or under beds, and for finding my way to restrooms during the night with as little disturbance as possible to others. It was one of the little things I had and needed but didn't know I needed at the time it was given to me. Every time I used it, I was grateful to Mr. Bill for looking out for me, because I never would have taken a flashlight. I thought it would be one more thing to carry. Plus I figured my cell phone would serve the purpose of finding my way in the dark.

Coleen and I had planned to walk to Estella, but during last night's pilgrims meal, someone recommended that we stay at the Casa Magica Albergue in Villatuerta. They had stayed there the previous year and thought it was one of the best albergues on the Camino. Villatuerta is about two miles (3.2km) before Estella. The appeal of getting another massage was incentive enough for Coleen and me to change our plans.

I had been working hard to keep the blisters on my heels from getting worse and so far the wrapping and taping had paid off; my feet were still sore, but it wasn't anything serious. Walking two miles less for the day would certainly help keep my feet from getting worse, or so I had hoped.

Coleen and I left the Albergue Jakue, but not before seeing a group of about fifteen female pilgrims outside the Jakue Hotel getting in a morning stretch before hitting the trail. Before the trail truly began, I crossed the famous Queen's Bridge where I stood with other pilgrims snapping photos and enjoying the beautiful scenery of the Rio Argo and distant mountains. It was a lovely way to begin a day of hiking in this beautiful Navarra Region of Spain. Like in the Rojas region, most of the fields in this region were covered with golden hay and sprouts of purple plants, red poppies, with bushes of yellow jasmine along the hiking path. The trail was relatively pleasant and easy on the feet since they were covered with much smaller rocks and gravel, compared to the larger rocks and boulders during the previous day's hike.

I could only imagine, but this area appeared to be an upscale region of the Camino. It was beautiful, breathtaking even. Farmers obviously had farming equipment that was necessary to manage vast acreage of hay fields and vineyards. The trail was open and scenic and clearly marked with yellow arrows on stone columns implanted in the ground. Some signs had encouraging notes placed on them by – I assumed – thoughtful pilgrims. One sign in particular, stood out for me. *Inner peace begins the moment you choose not to allow another person or event to control your emotions.* – Pema Chadron.

One thing about the Camino and walking it alone, the distance and mileage allow for long hours of time to just think. I hadn't thought much before this moment about my thoughts. Of course, there were the moments of overthinking about the pain, the trail, and could I actually complete the Camino. There were times when I thought about making it to the next destination, and then there was the fear of not being able to. Would I be physically able to make it the next town or village if no rooms were available? Other than those moments of uncertainty, I hadn't thought much about thinking. The little-typed sign left on the column made me do just that. Think.

Inner peace. What a concept. The idea of it made me think about happiness. As I walked, I thought about how the two differed. Inner peace and happiness. With no dictionary available to validate my understanding of inner peace, I tried to define it as best I could. I settled for this...*the ability to remain in a fairly peaceful state, even when threats of internal and external interferences exist.* I stopped, detached my stylist pen from my cell phone and wrote down my personal definition of inner peace. As soon as I was near Wi-Fi, I googled the term inner peace. *"Inner peace (or peace of mind) refers to a deliberate state of psychological or spiritual calm despite the potential of stressors."* Close enough, but the addition of 'spiritual' was worth adding it to my own definition. My adjusted definition became, *the ability to remain and maintain psychologically and spiritually calm, even when threats of internal and external interferences exist.*

What a beautiful thing to possess, inner peace. I wondered if I possessed it. My initial thought was, *No, I don't.* I live in a large urban environment and works in an urban school with urban problems like poverty and all the things that come with having students who live with limited resources and parents struggling to carve out a better life for themselves and their children. I work long pass my contracted hours, which is the only way to get required work done and to meet the academic needs of my students. I am also involved in community service activities. I have loved ones and friends whom I need in my life and who need me in theirs, and making it all happen takes dedication and participation. I need 'me' time; seriously need it and must have it. I read, I exercise – at least I try. I have a dog that depends on me. These were my thoughts about inner peace, and I realize without all the things I do and try to do, I probably would starve for inner peace. What I have, or what I think I have, isn't perfect, but I do know it's enough to keep me centered and purposeful. I accept that as my inner peace.

Happiness, on the other hand, seems to be a bit more challenging. At least I think it is. One day not long ago, I had a deep discussion with a dear friend about happiness. We talked at length about happiness and how to best define it. Near the end of a back-and-forward discussion, we concluded that each person is responsible for their own happiness. It sound good and righteous. The following day, my dear friend called back to continue the discussion. Happiness, we ended up agreeing, is fleeting; It's not always there, and when it is, it doesn't always last. Money can't buy it, it can't be planned, and it isn't promised. It's here today and gone tomorrow. Enjoy and treasure it while it's there.

Unlike inner peace, where a person can develop and maintain a sense of peace within, happiness is unpredictable. We are always in pursuit of it. To achieve it, conditions must be right, failures should be at a minimum, with basic needs like food, shelter and health in place. A bigger part of happiness is that you stand a better chance of obtaining it when you give it to others. In other words, you get what you put out. Deep thinking I know, but on the Camino, there was plenty of time for it.

Just before reaching the beautiful hilltop village of Cirauqui, I passed a gated cemetery. Through the iron fence, there were tall, ornate crosses placed on tombs and graves. A little farther on the trail, I noticed a couple of crosses in the ground with flowers around them, obviously put there as a tribute to someone who had passed away. Both were adoring ways in which people honored the deceased.

The village of Cirauqui with its incredible panoramic views was magical. Homes were adorned with blooming flowerbeds and matching wooden doors at the front of the house and the garage that I would love to have at my home. It was yet another village or town I passed without seeing residents. Not one. I started to wonder where the residents of these small villages worked. Did they drive to Pamplona? Was farming their sole financial resource? And, I wondered, where were the young people? Like many small towns in America, I wondered did young people grow up and move to larger cities to start families of their own?

Before leaving Cirauqui, I stopped at a local café and had lunch with a few other female pilgrims. They were friends, and all four were having difficulties with blisters and sore knees. Like Coleen and me, they too were planning to stay at the La Casa Magica in Villafuerta. They planned to stay for a couple of days to rest and heal.

I arrived at La Casa Magica tired and very sore. My feet hurt and I could tell that my blistered had become aggravated. I couldn't wait to register, get my assigned bed, and take a shower.

One thing about all albergues…every pilgrim is required to remove their hiking shoes at the entrance. Doing so helps keep floors free of dirt. My feet were sore and walking on the stone floors and stairs leading to rooms didn't help. The floors were beautiful, but I felt every step and couldn't wait to get off my feet.

I met Coleen in our assigned room as she was preparing to leave for her scheduled massage. She left while I unpacked and showered. We were lucky to have room with just the two of us. This was rare on the Camino. Unless pilgrims purchased a private hotel room, they were, more often than not, assigned to dorm-style room with a large number of single beds or bunks. Some albergues had multiple rooms with a number of beds in each while others had several rooms on multiple levels. The room Coleen and I were assigned to had four single beds with no bunks.

More than anything, I wanted to sit, relax and recover from the day's hike, but getting a massage was too good to pass up. The masseur was the same gentleman who checked me in; I assumed he is the owner of the albergue. He noticed the blister on my toe and for five extra euros he treated the new blister and checked the others to see how the healing was progressing. He used a pair of small scissors and sniped a portion of the raised skin. No needle and thread, no Compede, just the small incision to allow for drainage, and cotton and bandage for protection. The massage was great, and the method for treating my blisters is the one I would use during my remaining time on the Camino.

The best part of La Casa Magica was the outside quad area where pilgrims could do laundry, relax in a hammock, or soak tired feet in the small wading pool. The place had a spa feel to it. I met three women – one from Southern California – who were on their second and third night at the albergue. I liked walking and every morning, no matter how tired or sore I was, I wanted to be on the Camino trail. But if there were a place where I could stop to heal and rest, and spend an extra night or two, this would be it. The ladies and I sat and discussed injuries and our Camino experiences. We all had similar feet and knees injuries. We were all doing the Camino solo, and we were all fearless women determined to complete the journey, one way or another.

**** *Villatuerta* - *pretty, quaint village*

***** *Casa Magica Albergue* – *one of my favorite albergues, a perfect place to relax, heal and meditate.*

Villatuerta to Los Arcos

16.5 mi (26.5 km)

Waking up around 6:00am, the quiet duties of repacking backpacks and preparing feet for the day's journey made this morning like all others. Like every other morning, I felt the pain and the soreness, just less intense. I attributed it to the wonderful massage and a great night's sleep. Like all other mornings on the Camino, the pain and soreness would remain until after breakfast when I could take a much-needed 800m ibuprofen.

What was different about the start of this morning was how I felt. It may have been due to a combination of things: the massage, my body becoming acclimated to averaging a half marathon everyday, the La Casa Magica, and the Camino itself. Whatever the case, I felt energized and spiritually alive.

I had awakened a few times during the night, and while Coleen slept, I opened my mini IPAD and read some of the inspirational and motivational quotes and saying I had placed in a file for those moments when I felt discouraged.

One quote in particular caught my attention. *Sometimes the smallest step in the right direction ends up being the biggest step of your life. Tip toe if you must* (author unknown). I reread the words and refocused on the big picture of my journey: making my way to Santiago, one step at a time.

As a pilgrim, this was my moment that the constant pain became secondary. With the remaining distance to Santiago and uncertain terrain, I suspected pain would always be present to some degree. Today there was less of it and more spiritual and mindful awareness. I felt good.

Coleen and I were up and out on the trail by 7:00am. As she and I often did, we walked together long enough to share morning breakfast and discuss the day's journey and destination. Soon after she was gone from my sight. While reviewing John Brierley's guide over dinner the night before, I noticed there were two routes to Los Arcos. Both peaked about the same, around 720m (2362ft). The Practical Path had a steeper incline, so I decided to take the alternative route. I felt good, but the last thing I wanted was to struggle with a steep incline, not if there was another option.

The climb on the alternate route was gradual and pleasant on my still-sore feet. As the day progressed, the overcasted morning skies cleared, bringing the heat. Thankfully, the inclining part of the trail weaved through a shady, cool forest. Like always, I was far slower than other pilgrims I met along the way. Fellow pilgrims always seemed to pass me; I rarely passed anyone. I was slow, plus I still stopped often to catch my breath, take photos, or just to absorb the beauty of my surroundings. There was something so magical and simplistic about the Camino. The beauty of it never got old.

Walking alone was no big deal. I was exceptionally slow, and being on my own was fine with me. I enjoyed the forest path. The shade made it easier. I cleared the forest area without seeing another pilgrim. The path after the clearing had me wondering if I had somehow taken a wrong turn. I saw no one, not a single hiker during this stretch. One thing I learned about the Camino was it wouldn't take long to discover you were on the wrong path.

In preparation for hiking the Camino, I read books, studied its history, studied guides, and followed Facebook groups to learn as much as I could about it. I learned about hiking the trails alone. No matter whom I met or how much I enjoyed sharing meals and conversations with other pilgrims, I knew without a doubt, completing the Camino was mine to do alone.

As nervous as I was about possibly taking a wrong turn, the scenery was breathtaking. The forest area cleared to reveal panoramic valley views of tiny farms and villages. Like always, I stopped to take pictures and to catch my breath. The decent was the same. I didn't see another pilgrim.

Back on leveled ground, I crossed a highway and saw a sign saying 9k (5.6 miles) to Los Arcos. I thought Los Arcos would have been a little closer, but it was not to be. And the heat soon became another factor.

From the 9km sign, there was intense sun without a cloud in the sky. I wasn't prepared; I have no sunscreen and a limited amount of water. 1.5 miles (2.5k) after the 9k sign, Eduardo's Food Truck appeared, and not a moment too soon. The heat had me fatigued and worried about dehydration. I was so happy that the food truck was there offering snacks and refreshments to weary pilgrims. I met a mother and her pregnant daughter from London. They were hoping to get to Burgos, but they were having second thoughts. A spider had bitten the daughter the night before, and the mark was something to worry about, especially with the pregnancy. The bite mark had swollen beyond any insect bite I'd ever seen. The mother was rightfully concerned about the health of her daughter and unborn grandchild. The three of us sat for about an hour hydrating and talking about England and the United States.

The longer we sat, the more I dreaded the rest of the walk, so I said farewells and offered well-wishes to the mother and daughter and started on my way. There was still no shade, and the sun was now directly overhead. There was one tree on this path that offered a small amount of shade. I did my best to stand under it, but it wasn't enough to shade my entire body. As I stood, I saw a copy of John Brierley's A *Pilgrim's Guide To The Camino de Santiago* with *free* written on it. Since I had been using a digital copy, I picked it up and took it with me. The paperback guide became my constant companion on the Camino. I considered it a nice, much-appreciated gift from the Camino. *The Camino Provides.*

This was the day I came to appreciate that precious moment on the Camino when your destination appears before you. Sometimes it's sudden – you look up, and it's there. Other times, you're guided by signs and motivated by anticipation, or you can see it off in the distance.

I arrived at the Casa De Alberta in Los Arcos weary and sun-beaten. I showered, washed my clothes and could have easily gone to bed. I was exhausted and the last thing I wanted to do was to go out and eat, but I needed food for energy. I found a quick bite at a neighboring restaurant. The running river next to the albergue was inviting and too good to pass up, so I sat on the bank and ate my food while I soaked my feet in the cool water.

I shared a room with Coleen, Laura from Canada, Antonio from Puerto Rico, and Shelley from Great Britain. There was one moment in the room when only Laura and I were there; the others were out enjoying a pilgrims meal. Laura and I were engrossed in a conversation about our respective countries when she posed a question I wasn't prepared for. She asked, *What question are you trying to seek an answer to?* I hadn't heard the question before, but I suspected that by the end of the Camino, I should or hoped to have an answer. At that moment, I just didn't know.

Later I sat outside and enjoyed the sights. I met three people on their third Camino and I couldn't help but wonder, what is it about this place – that isn't easy by any stretch of the imagination – that keeps some people returning for more? Why do people endure the blisters, sore knees, injuries, and intense weather conditions to do the Camino again and again? Like with Laura's question, it was something to ponder.

***** **Los Arcos** – great place to stop and relax.*

***** **Casa du la Abuela** – friendly staff, great location next to the river, great nearby restaurants*

Los Arcos to Logrono

17.3 mi (27.8 km)

The day began with another solemn morning of pilgrims prepping for the day's hike. The weather was to be a repeat of the day before – hot. The terrain was the same; little shade and wide open fields. Coleen and I had decided to leave earlier than our usual start time. We were out and on the path by 6:00am to get a jump-start on the heat. According to the guide, the path wouldn't be difficult, only one moderately steep 100m (328ft) climb around the 6-mile (10km) mark.

With eight days behind us, Coleen and I hadn't had a problem with finding beds. I knew my good fortune came from having her around. She was a fast walker and was still able to secure a bed for me without a problem when she arrived at our destination. On several occasions during dinner, a few coupled pilgrims I spoke with had also been able to reserve a bed for the slower partner, provided the later person checked in by a certain time, usually by 3:00pm or 4:00pm. As late as I had been yesterday, I went to bed grateful for Coleen, her youth and her long, strong legs.

The early morning prep routine allowed me time to assess my blisters. I didn't have any new ones, but the two on my heels were bothering me. I gave up on using Compede. Instead, I moisturized my feet each night and morning and used only cotton and tape before I started the day.

My right knee wasn't doing too badly – no swelling, no extreme pain, thanks to the 800m ibuprofen I took after every breakfast. The daily stiff-legged penguin walk was always there until the medication kicked in and my limbs loosened.

After breakfast, Coleen and I were on our way. She was soon out of sight, and I walked for a brief while with Laura from Toronto. Laura was talkative and friendly. She and I shared information about our lives, and for the first time since I began my Camino, I engaged in an extended conversation about politics. Not that I was against it, I just wasn't ready to hear the opinion of others about the political climates of the world. I had gotten enough at home. Plus, it had never come up until now.

Laura was interested in my perspective on the United States presidential campaign. I, on the other hand, wanted to hear about the fairly new prime minister, health insurance, and the Canadian job market. She hoped one day to visit the United States. A popular destination for Canadians – according to her – was Las Vegas, Nevada.

One thing about conversations on the Camino, they felt honest, comfortable, never forced. I appreciated whenever I got the opportunity to talk with people from other parts of the world. Our differences paled in comparison to our similarities. (When I returned home from the Camino, my head and heart were filled with the experiences, the many languages, and getting to talk with beautiful, spiritual people from different countries and continents.)

I slowed down a bit after Laura joined a group she had walked with before, and for the first time since I started this journey, I walked ahead of a group of men and women. I'm sure the ibuprofen had something to do with how I was feeling. I also knew I was getting stronger. My faster pace had me smiling.

The trail and the weather were not much different from the day before. The moderate hill wasn't bad, and I was alone by the time I climbed it. I could see a few lone groups ahead of me, but no one passed me. The most memorable moment of this day was beautiful Viana, a small medieval town I later discovered was a main stopover for pilgrims during the 15th Century. I wished I could have stayed overnight, but Coleen and I had decided to end the day's hike in Logrono. The short time I'd been on the Camino was enough to know I preferred staying in smaller villages, yet I found it nice to occasionally experience larger towns and cities like Logrono. Though it would have been nice to explore the historical church in Viana.

I arrived in Logrono after six hours on the trail. Like yesterday, I was fatigued and weather-beaten from the sun.

When I arrived, Coleen had showered and finished her laundry; her routine included Facetiming her sons who were staying with their grandparents. I appreciated that each day we were together, she patiently waited for me to shower and complete my laundry so we could have dinner together. We both looked forward to getting out and enjoying Logrono.

Logrono was a beautiful city, and the albergue was in the center of shops and restaurants all mixed with a good share of pilgrims and tourist. We decided to walk around the downtown Logrono, plus I needed to find an ATM and get cash.

One important decision all pilgrims need to make when doing the Camino is how to deal with money. Only larger hotels accepted credit cards, while albergues, hostels, cafes and most restaurants only accepted cash – euros. In researching the Camino, I read about the different manners people dealt with cash. Some carried enough cash to last the entire Camino, while a few opened bank accounts in Spain to avoid the international fees of converting homeland currency to euros. And some, like me, carried enough cash to last until they could find an ATM for cash.

Money was one of those things I agonized over as I prepared for my trip. I feared taking all my money with me. What if it were stolen, or I accidentally left it somewhere? I would have been devastated. I thought at one time about opening a bank account in Spain, but I never considered it seriously enough to get it done. I left home with a little over 400 euros and about 60 U.S. dollars. The dollars I kept stashed away would be used when I return to the States. When I landed in Europe, it was all cash and all euros.

Hiking the Camino is doable for people from all walks of life because it doesn't take a lot of money. I found food inexpensive, and the albergues I chose cost from seven to fifteen euros. My biggest expenses were the few hotels I chose. The only added costs were the items I bought in pharmacies like medical tape, and other products for my feet. I also purchased ibuprofen cream for my knee.

To get euros from an ATM, I had to bite the bullet on the high-cost transfer fees – about 30 dollars each of the three times I got cash. On the average, I spent 15 to 30 euros a day, depending on the cost of albergue and whether I had a pilgrims meal or grabbed something from a local café. During my 35 days on the Camino, I had seven pilgrim meals. For me, the meal was too much food, and it was served too late, usually at 7:00pm. Depending on the albergue and region, the meal usually consisted of potatoes, salad/vegetables, chicken or beef, a dessert and unlimited red wine, and cost between 9 to 15 euros, a bargain considering all the food served. I enjoyed the small local bars and cafes where I could get a burger, tapas or a bocadillo (sandwich) and wine for a few euros.

During our night in Logrono, Coleen and I chose to eat at a local bar not far from where we were staying. We later sat on a bench outside of the albergue and people-watched.

***** ***Logrono*** – *beauty city, great for touring*

**** ***Hotel Entresuenos*** – *centrally located with an albergue for pilgrims*

Logrono to Najera

18 miles (28.9km)

It was to be another sunny, very warm day, so after last night's dinner and planning meeting to determine today's destination, Coleen and I were in our bunks a little earlier than usual. Normally, we turned in between 9:30pm and 10:00pm. It may have seemed early, but after walking six to eight hours a day, neither of us could stay awake past 10:00pm. In fact, most pilgrims turned in early; a few mostly younger pilgrims stayed awake long enough to enjoy some of the Camino's nightlife. Strangely, it was always daylight when I fell asleep and I was surprised to learn that sunsets happened around 10:30pm during the spring and early summer on the Camino.

Coleen and I were on the trail by 6:30am with daylight on the horizon. As we reached the outskirts of Logrono, we passed through a tunnel with a map of the Camino painted on one of its walls. The sheer size of it put the journey to Santiago in perspective. It gave me a more realistic idea on the journey.

This was day ten, and I had hiked 119 miles (187k). I was happy that I had made it this far, and at the same time, it had me anxious that I still had a great distance to travel.

Coleen was off in the distance and I was alone with my thoughts. I wondered how I would feel in another week, another 2 weeks, or during my final week on the Camino. I wondered how it would feel to make it to the end, to stand in front of the Santiago Cathedral. I wondered about my body and how it would hold up to the day-to-day walking, climbing, and more climbing. What condition would it be in? I feared that 36 days wouldn't be enough time. I thought about the 9 days it had taken to walk 119 miles (187k) at an average of 13.2 miles a day. I also wondered if my pace was too slow. I knew I was overthinking, but I was legitimately concerned. With the city lights of Logrono behind me, I enjoyed the short walk along the small riverbed along the trail.

When I was a young girl growing up in urban Chicago, my parents were serious about discipline. I was expected to do as I was told without thought or question. Or else. The consequence for disobedience was swift and often physical. The 'else' was a sometimes a branch from a tree with the leaves removed. I remember the group of trees in our yard that I and most of my friends fondly called 'switch trees.' And here I stood in Spain, 4158 miles (6692k) from where I grew up, standing next to a tree that caused childhood memories to resurface. I had to smile at the thought.

I walked into Navarette – another beautiful, historical town – alone. I stopped for lunch and to rest my tired feet.

After eating and rehydrating, I visited the 16th Century Church of the Assumption. As always, I lit a candle and stamped my passport.

The Camino de Santiago wasn't a religious journey for me, but I loved the churches and never tired of going in, lighting a candle, and saying a prayer. I saw the churches as valued symbols of the traditions and cultures of the Spanish people. I appreciated the sounds of church bells each morning and every night.

Coleen and I were back on the trail determined to make it to Najera before the hottest part of the day, and at noon, it was already pretty hot. The trail continued to be wide open, and from a higher elevation, the views of rolling vineyards and scattered homes were clear for miles. There was thankfully a food truck on the open part of the trail where no other food places were available. Standing there, getting something to drink were Antonio from Puerto Rico, Sarah from Italy, and Noah from Brazil. Next to the truck was an added bonus; the owner had a table and chairs covered by a canopy. It was a nice and much-needed rest stop.

I liked Najera immediately. The town had a population of less than 10,000 people according to John Brierley's guide, yet it was more like a city. Coleen and I stayed at the Puerta de Najera, an albergue that overlooked the Rio Yalde. There were a number of restaurants and cafes nearby. This was one of the few times I saw pilgrims eating and mingling with locals. It was a lovely place, and I welcomed the opportunity to watch children run around and play ball along the riverbank. It was also the first time I ate paella (a Spanish rice dish with seafood, veggies and meat) on the Camino. Before going in for the evening, I left Coleen and walked down to the river to soak my weary, burning feet.

***** ***Najera*** – *beautiful town, great food and wine*

**** ***Puerta de Najera Albergue*** – *the rooms were small and crowded with beds, but the albergue was clean and airy*

Najera to Santa Domingo

13.2 miles (21.3km)

After repacking and prepping feet for the day's journey, Coleen and I left the albergue and were happy to discover from one of the other pilgrims that the day, although sunny, would be cooler. It was daybreak and the first order of business, as always, was to find breakfast. We walked a very flat 3.8 miles (6.2km) before finding a café. There weren't many stops on this route so the cooler temperature would be welcomed.

I learned from a few English speaking Spaniards that Spain is divided into regions: Navarra, Rioja, Castilla Y Leon, and Galicia. The largest is Castillo Y Leon, and the smallest region is Rioja. There was something different about the Rioja region. Maybe it was the soil, the climate – I don't know, but it was my favorite region for wine and food, especially the wine. On average, a nice fill glass of wine cost 1 to 2 euros, no more. I assumed the wines came from local vineyards, but there was a rich, heavier body to the Rioja wines I tasted.

Houses in this region appeared more modern, more expensive, and larger with rich-looking matching garages, front doors, and beautiful shutters. I didn't see any farm animals – no cows, elk, horses. Vineyards appeared to be the industry of Rojas.

I felt good as I walked. I knew my body was getting stronger. I still relied heavily on my hiking poles – I couldn't imagine covering the many miles without them. They took pressure off my blistered feet, and they helped me maneuver the ever-present rocks and small boulders I walked on during my time on the Camino. Rocks were always present in open fields, and when climbing and descending mountains, provided needed traction. Wet or dry, hiking up and down a mountain would spell disaster without them to help stabilize footing.

With my body now better adapted to walking, this was the first day I spent most of my time hiking with other pilgrims. I walked almost the entire distance with Antonio, Sarah, and Noah. I was able to walk without much pain from my sore knee or my blisters, thanks to the ibuprofen. We laughed about pain, snoring pilgrims, and other Camino experiences. Both Antonio and Sarah had done the Camino before. We shared family backgrounds and what the Camino meant to each of us, personally and spiritually. Sarah was twenty-eight and was born in the Middle East. She spoke four languages, Portuguese, Italian, English, and Spanish. I was envious; I came to Spain with basic knowledge of Spanish, just enough to get by. It was amazing that so many European I met spoke three or more languages, while I relied on basic words and a few phrases in Spanish.

One of the most interesting areas of the day's hike was the golf course about halfway to Santa Domingo. By the time we made it to the golf course, only Antonio and I were together. Sarah and Noah were behind and didn't want to stop for food. The golf course was surrounded by hundreds of apartments, and I wondered if some corporation had intended to modernize the Camino and capitalize on its popularity and beauty. More unusual than the many buildings and units was that most of them appeared to be unoccupied, never lived in. Apart from the few people I saw going on and off the golf course, and the workers in the restaurant, the place was like a ghost town.

Antonio and I stopped at the restaurant where we were the only patrons. We sat and each of us ordered water, a beer and a ham and queso bocadillo. I had some very memorable meals on the Camino, like the times I ate Puella, great burgers, and tapas, but this ham and queso bocadillo was one of the best I'd ever eaten. Antonio and I raved about it for the entire day. It was that good.

The openness and vast fields resumed on the descent from Redecilla. The sun was blaring, but Antonio and I were spared from overheating by the pleasant, gentle breeze. I had stopped in a few pharmacies for foot care products: tape, cotton, Mercurochrome, moisturizers, and creams. The last time was in Logrono where I picked up another tube of 35sp sunscreen. While my face, arms, and my legs were a couple of shades darker already, the back of my neck was taking a beating. One purchase I wish I'd made in preparation for the Camino was a sun hat with a longer flap in the back to cover my neck. I wore a cap that did a good job of shielding the sun from my face, but I started to worry that my neck would burn from the constant exposure since the sun was always at my back. To help with the sun-on-my-neck situation, I wore my neck gaiter everyday, but I was envious of pilgrims who wore sun hats. About halfway to Santa Domingo, I stopped and applied another generous layer of sunscreen on my neck arms and legs.

This was the first day that I'd spent a significant amount of time with Antonio. I enjoyed him. He was easy to talk to, and since I knew very little about Puerto Rico, I pumped him for information about his life there. He was hopeful for his struggling homeland. He tried to remain positive about its economic uncertainties. We talked about our love for hiking, and he invited me to visit and hike one of the rainforests on the island.

This was Antonio's second Camino. Three years prior, he completed the journey with a group from different parts of the world, all who paid a professional travel company to plan their trips from beginning to end. The company also arranged for luggage and backpack transportation from one destination to the next, all the way to Santiago. Though he was traveling solo this time, he booked this trip through the same travel company.

I asked Antonio how his family, mainly his wife felt about him being away for five weeks to walk the Camino.

She was fine with it. It appeared the Camino de Santiago is a popular vacation destination in Puerto Rico. He and a good friend hiked regularly. In fact, Antonio told me his friend was somewhere on the Camino. The two of them left at different times and planned to meet in a day or so.

We arrived in Santo Domingo mid-afternoon. The previous night, Coleen and I decided to stay at separated albergues in Santa Domingo. She would be staying with two ladies she met on the trail. They had bonded over conversations about travel and other similar interests. The three of them particularly connected over the idea of renting bikes and biking a portion of the Camino. With the exception of day one, this is the first day Coleen and I would be staying in separate albergues. It wasn't a big deal. I was completely supportive of her finding new people and interest. To me, that was one of the true beauties of doing the Camino solo – enjoying it to the fullest with ALL the beautiful people who came along, and doing it without feeling obligated to another person. When we talked about it at bedtime, I got the impression she was hurting a bit more than she cared to admit, and on the Camino, everyone hurt to some degree – stiffness, knee pain, back pain, feet issues – so complaining more than likely would fall on deaf ears. Not much sympathy was given when almost every other pilgrim dealt with some degree of pain of their own.

This night, I chose to stay where Antonio was staying. It was my first municipal albergue experience. Municipal albergues are larger facilities with more beds to a room and cost less than the private albergues I normally preferred.

Since I began the Camino – with the exception of SJPdP, Orission, and Roncesvalles – I had spent between 10-15 euros for a bed at private albergues. A bed at the Albergue Casa de la Cofradia del Santo in Santo Domingo cost 7 euros.

The way albergues work, at least in my experience, if you sign in with a friend, partner or spouse, one person was given a lower bunk, the other received the upper bunk. Coleen and I had traveled together from the beginning, and since she was always the first to arrive at the albergue, she received the lower bunk, and because she told the albergue I was coming and I was traveling with her, I was always assigned the bunk above her. The travel company had arranged Antonio's trip, so an albergue would know he traveled solo. I signed in solo also and it was the first time I slept in a lower bunk. You'd have to experience climbing up a bunk ladder with a tired body and sore feet to understand my joy of having a lower bunk. I was elated.

It was another evening that I wasn't hungry, but I needed food to fuel my body. Antonio, and Arturo – also from Puerto, were going out to eat and insisted on bringing me something back. When they returned with an extra burger, I forced myself out of bed to go the kitchen area and eat.

This albergue had about 140 bunks in several large rooms. Antonio, Arturo and I were assigned to a room with about twenty bunks. Larger rooms meant an increased number of snorers. This was the first night I used my earplugs.

I had read numerous books and followed Facebook pages where people wrote about the horrors of snoring on the Camino. I brought along two types of earplugs: an inexpensive foam pair, the other made of earwax that came in a cute little tin container. This night, I opted for the inexpensive ones. Whenever the level of snoring dictated earplugs during my time on the Camino, I used the foam ones and they worked just fine.

***** *Santo Domingo* – *great small village, I didn't get out to explore it, but I liked what I saw*

***** *Albergue Casa de la Cofradia del Santo* – *my only municipal albergue, I loved it, rooms had large windows to allow an evening breeze, also had large, clean restrooms*

Santo Domingo to Belorado

14 miles (22.5km)

I awoke this morning knowing that this could very well be the first day I would begin my day without Coleen. I believed – even felt – she had stayed nearby and that I would see her at some point on the trail, hopefully for breakfast at a nearby café. We had already mapped out our next few stops. I was sure she'd stop in Belorado then Ages, but we hadn't discussed where we would stay.

The hike to Belorado was pleasant and leveled – a nice relief on the blisters I now had on both feet. There were still rocks, everyday, all day, large and small to contend with. Today I was grateful that there were no major hills and mountains to climb. Antonio, Arturo and I stopped in Granon for breakfast. We sat outside on my request, as I hoped to see Coleen and a few other pilgrims I knew.

One thing to remember about hiking the Camino de Santiago; you will meet people along the way who you will come to care about. When the routine of seeing them is broken, you can't help but be concerned, and I was concerned about Coleen. After eating and resting, Antonio, Arturo and I decided to move on and walk slowly in case Coleen was close behind.

The weather remained pleasant, not hot, but sunny. Unlike yesterday, there were four villages between Santo Domingo and Belorado: Granon, Redecilla, Valorea, and Villamayor. We could stop for beverages and food as many times as needed.

About half of the hike was done along the side of a highway. While researching the Camino de Santiago, I read some people's complaints about walking along highways. Most didn't like it. As an American who lives in a state that was rated as having the worst highway traffic in the United States, I thought walking alongside highways of the Camino would be a problem and it would take away from the true spirit of the journey. The highways trails along the Camino were nothing like what I was used to. They were quiet in comparison. Occasionally, there were a few passing cars and a pickup truck or two, but nothing I found too overwhelming or distracting from the journey. There were times when I walked from one wheat field or vineyard to the next with nothing in between, so the occasional trek by or on a highway wasn't a problem for me.

Leaving Granon meant leaving behind the La Rioja region of Spain. We were now in the Castillo Y Leon region, the largest region of Spain.

I was grateful for the leveled terrain and more than pleased with how my body was responding to walking 6 to

8 hours everyday. I no longer had to stop on the side of the trail just to catch my breath.

Antonio and Arturo were just ahead of me when we arrived in Villamayor around 2:00pm. I was feeling a little pain in my knee, and when the two guys stopped in one of the cafes, I chose to walk on. This was the last village before Belorado, and I didn't want to stop. I decided to walk on at a slow pace until the men caught up with me. When they did catch me, I was a little surprised by Antonio's reaction. Apparently, he was annoyed with me for not stopping, or maybe it was because I didn't say I was walking on. Arturo was OK, but Antonio was quiet and distant.

The reaction, for a very brief moment, had me second-guessing my decision to continue to walk after they had stopped. I wondered if I was supposed to consider what was best for others, or was this Camino – my Camino – about what was best for me? I didn't react or respond to Antonio's noticeable irritation with me, but it caused me to pause and reevaluate the Camino experience. I didn't want to depend on anyone else. Don't get me wrong; if someone I met was in trouble and needed help in any way, I would assist them however I could. But I was a solo hiker, and I depended on my gut instincts and how my body felt to determine the choices I made.

During my time on the Camino, I came across a few ladies who started out solo but were unexpectedly joined by other hikers, particularly men interested in them. The women ended up having to ditch the men by leaving earlier or joining other groups just to get away from them. I'd read and seen video documentaries about men and women being crushed because people suddenly wanted to walk alone. This wasn't the situation with Antonio, but I did come to the conclusion that I wasn't going to get caught up in anyone's expectations of how I did the Camino, how I did *my* Camino.

By the time the three of us walked into Belorado, conversations and mannerisms between Antonio and me were back to normal and the miscommunication forgotten. We checked into the El Caminante Albergue. I showered, did my laundry and decided to go out and find a quick bite to eat. There were a number of pilgrims here that I knew besides Antonio and Arturo. They wanted to do the 7:00pm pilgrims meal and I agreed to join them. For the moment I wanted a glass of wine and something quick to eat. I walked around the quaint village half-hoping to see Coleen or some of the other pilgrims who might know where she was staying. I was starting to miss her, and more than anything, I wanted our end-of-the-day discussion about the day's hike, the beautiful scenery, the aches and pains. The last time I saw her, she was having problems with blisters and knee pain. I wanted to know how she was doing. I wanted to tell her about Antonio being annoyed with me. I saw one pilgrim who knew Coleen. He hadn't seen her, so I hobbled to one of the local cafes for tapas and wine. On my way back, I stopped at the beautiful cathedral where I sat awhile and got a stamp for my passport.

This pilgrims meal was one of my favorites. Antonio, Arthur and I shared a table with Joe from Germany and Sarah from Italy. The food was simple, but very good, and the conversation and laughter among people who shared a love for the Camino was priceless.

I went to bed (a bottom bunk, thankfully) thinking about the fascinating people of this world. As an African American woman, I've experienced so much more joy than I have pain. I've experienced friendships with men and women from all races, ethnicities, cultural and political views, so I'm never uncomfortable around different people, not unless I get a vibe of unfriendliness. If I do, I quickly remove myself for the situation. Again, it's my gut and intuition that I trust. Sitting with a man from Germany, a Muslim woman from Italy, and two men from Puerto Rico was a joy. We each shared our ambitions and why we walked the Camino. We talked briefly about the political climate of the world. It was one of my favorite evenings. Later, sleep didn't come easily. The people of the small village apparently knew how to have a good time. From the window next to my bed, I could hear the Saturday night festivities coming from the village square. I wished I had enough energy to stay up later and experience how the locals enjoyed life.

PART II

The Middle

Belorado to Ages

18 miles (29km).
The Day That Tested
My Strength & Mental Fortitude

Never since I started the Camino did I once think about giving up. In spite of the blisters and sore knee, every morning I awoke excited about hitting the trail, ready to enjoy the incredible scenery and all the Camino has to offer. I always looked forward to seeing pilgrims I knew and meeting new ones.

I awoke around 5:00am needing a trip to the restroom. Some pilgrims were already awake and prepared to leave. Antonio was in the lower bunk next to mine. He was lying in bed looking at his phone. When I returned from the restroom, he shared his sad news.

Antonio had been on the phone all night with his wife, working on plans for him to return home. His elderly father had fallen out of bed and was now in the hospital. During his conversation with his wife, the decision was made for him to abandon the Camino and immediately return to Puerto Rico. Needless to say, Antonio was disappointed, but knew his family needed him and returning home was the right thing to do.

During the night, instead of sleeping, Antonio had made arrangements to fly out of Leon that evening. He planned to take a taxi to Burgos as soon as possible then take a two-hour bus ride to Leon. He was so sad, I'm sure for his family situation, and for having to end his journey on the Camino.

While talking with Antonio as he packed, I made an idiotic decision that could have derailed my own Camino. I don't know why I did it. Maybe it was losing touch with Coleen and now Antonio, but I decided to ride to Burgos with Antonio. In my mind, I would go to Burgos and spend a day or two resting my knee and allowing my blisters to heal. At the time, I thought it was a great idea.

After packing and seeing all the other pilgrims off, Antonio and I walked through the village square and found a taxi that would take us to Burgos. The distance from Belorado to Burgos was 31.2 miles (45.3k). For the record, had I not left with Antonio, I would have been on the trail hiking 15 miles (24.2k) to San Juan. The following day, I would have hiked 16.2 miles (26.1k) to Burgos. Instead of taking two days to get to Burgos, I was going to arrive by taxi within the next hour.

From the taxi, I noticed we were traveling on the highway adjacent to the Camino trail. I couldn't help but feel a twinge of guilt for not being there. The taxi ride felt wrong. Yes, I was sore, and I was dealing with painful blisters and an achy knee, but I was discovering something about myself. Pain was a part of my Camino journey, and it would be there, and in spite of the pain, I was doing OK. My body was adjusting, acclimating to walking long distances everyday. I looked forward to each day on the trail.

On this day, the snap judgment to forgo two days of hiking was a decision I regretted immediately. However, as the saying goes, *The Camino provides.* Two things happened that forced me to sit down and seriously consider my next move.

First, while riding to Burgos, Antonio told me something I hadn't remembered. He informed me of the rules for getting a Compostela in Santiago. A Compostela is the document given to pilgrims who complete the required distance to Santiago. The least distance a pilgrim must travel is 88.7 miles (142.8k) from Sarria to Santiago. One of the stipulations is that your pilgrim passport must not have any gaps. My last stamp was Belorado. If my next stamp came from Burgos, there would be a gap, and there was no way I could justify covering 31.2 miles (45.3k) in one day. I still could have gotten a Compostela from the distance of Sarria to Santiago, but I wanted my Compostela to reflect my start in SJPdP.

When Antonio told me about the rules, I remembered reading about some people who arrived at the pilgrims office in Santiago for their Compostela only to be denied because they weren't able to explain walking great distances in short amounts of time. Antonio's news was depressing, but I was grateful to him for telling me.

We arrived in Burgos, wished each other well and said our goodbyes, then he was off to the bus station to take the bus ride to Leon. He recommended that I stay in the albergue where he was supposed to stay for the night. The taxi driver drove the short distance to the albergue, and to my surprise, it was closed. Most albergues don't open until 3:00pm or 4:00pm. There was a hotel just down the block. I went there and reserved a room for one night with the option for a second. I couldn't check in until 2:00pm, so I left my backpack and went out to find food.

I was sitting at a lovely little café in the tourist area of Burgos enjoying a café con leche, a croissant, and orange juice when I realized the worse. This was the second thing that forced me to reflect on my next move. I had left my hiking shoes at the El Caminante Albergue in Belorado. It was the worse feeling ever. I couldn't believe it. I finished my breakfast and seriously thought about my next move. I had several options; I could find a store and buy a new pair of hiking shoes. I paid $150 (126 euros) for my Merrel Moab Waterproof Hiking Shoes.

There were well broken in, and I liked them. The idea of breaking in a new pair of shoes while on the trail didn't seem right, especially now that I was dealing with painful blisters. Of course, I would buy new shoes if I had to, but the other option was to go back to Belorado. Bottom line, I needed my shoes, and another advantage of going back, it would put me back on track for getting my Compostela.

After an hour or so of sitting, thinking and scolding myself for this morning's snappy, bonehead decision to follow Antonio to Burgos, I went back to the hotel, changed my reservation to the following day, and went out again to find a taxi stand. The first driver to stop didn't want to drive to Belorado. The second one did for the flat fee of 50 euros.

I made it back to the El Caminante Albergue in Belorado, retrieved my hiking shoes, and took off on the trail. I was mentally exhausted from the ordeal. I had taken ibuprofen in the taxi. I didn't think much about blisters or my sore knee.

The predicament forced for me to dig deep within myself to find and maintain the mental strength and willpower to get through the hike and over the mishap.

Thankfully, there were plenty of stops along the trail, and I stopped every time I could, sometimes for food and a much-needed café con leche (I had three over the course of the day), one time for a cold beer, and a time or two just to rest and hydrate. Welcomed trees shaded much of the path. After a slight mountain climb, the path was more opened to the sky, and the sun shone brightly.

I was still feeling a bit overwhelmed from events of the day, but after reaching my intended destination, San Juan, I decided to go on to the next town of Ages. I had stuffed my daypack with something to sleep in and another pair of legging and tee shirt for the next day. Physically, I wasn't feeling too bad, considering, and hiking the additional 2.2 miles (3.6k) would shorten the next day's hike into Burgos. I had gained enough experience on the Camino to understand that adding the extra miles at the end of the day, especially when I felt strong enough, would be beneficial the following day. More mileage now meant fewer later.

***** **Ages** – *a nice village to stop in, I wanted to get out and explore it, but I was too tired.*

***** **San Rafael Albergue** – *loved it, older facility with a friendly, kindhearted staff*

The following morning, when I was leaving for the trail, one of my hiking poles was missing. At every albergue, hiking poles and hiking shoes are kept in an area near the entrance. With the in-and-out traffic from the Camino trail and villages, it's a logical solution for keeping facility floors clean. It could have been accidental that someone picked up the wrong pole, so I didn't worry about it. Maybe one pole would have worked for me, but I didn't want to chance it if I didn't have to. I depended on two hiking poles to support my arthritic knee. I took a chance and asked the owner if he had an extra pole. Without hesitation, he opened the door to a nearby closet and told me to pick one. It was one of the many moments on the Camino that I was overwhelmed by the kindness of people. *The Camino provides.*

Ages to Burgos

14 miles (22.5km)

This was the first day of my journey that I'd left an albergue alone. I didn't know any of the other pilgrims I'd roomed with. Since I had reservations at the Burgos hotel, I didn't have to worry about the chance of not getting a bed. I could take my time covering the 14 miles (22.5k) to Burgos.

While Antonio and I were riding to Burgos yesterday, besides the information he shared about getting a Compostela in Santiago, I learned about the agency he used and the travel details of his Camino. All his hotels and albergues had been reserved, and his luggage was picked-up every day – like mine – and taken to the next location. He carried a large daypack on the trail. His larger luggage had his many changes of clothes, additional shoes, and snack foods. When we left Belorado, Antonio gave me two boxes of trail mix. He also passed on his list of reserved albergues and hotels. From this day on, I followed the list and stayed where Antonio would have. This was the fourth day that I had checked my backpack because of knee pain and my concerns about crossing mountains with the twelve additional pounds. I carried only my small daypack. I carried my sandals to change into when necessary, water, snack food, medication and a foot repair kit with surgical scissors, tape, and bandages. This was the day, I decided, that I would never carry my large backpack again. I would use the company Antonio used.

There were clear advantages and disadvantages to checking my backpack. The advantage was not carrying the extra weight. My knee was still sore, but nowhere near as sore as when I walked all day with the additional weight of a backpack. The disadvantage was not having all my supplies with me. If I ever needed to stop before my intended destination, I would have had a problem. Checking my backpack meant I had to go where it had been sent. Regardless of the potential problem, I sent my backpack forward all the way to Santiago. I never regretted it or had a problem. Most albergues are stocked with envelopes from transportation companies. On my way out, I grabbed a few envelopes to use once I got the Burgos.

On the trail, I took a chance and decided to take the Castanures Path along the River Arlanzon. The trail wasn't well marked. In fact, the further I got into Burgos, I didn't see any marks at all. This was one of those 'gut' moments when I decided to continue. I knew I was traveling along the side of Burgos city limits; I didn't want to walk on city streets if I didn't have to. It was one of the most beautiful paths with its mix of unique architecture, peaceful parks, and a running river. Knowing I was in Burgos and also knowing the hotel was near the cathedral, I figured I was close, and if it were farther than expected, I would take a taxi to the hotel.

In my life experiences, I have found that having a second sense, being intuitive – along with that gut instinct – always served me well, especially in unhealthy or unfamiliar surroundings. Being intuitive and having endurance, I believe, are essential for doing the Camino, especially doing it solo. I don't think anyone – man or woman, young or old – should ever get so comfortable that natural defenses and concerns for safety are ignored. Stay vigilant. If it feels wrong, do something about it. Not that something, anything couldn't go wrong, especially something like yesterday's snafu. The idea of getting past the bad and enjoying the breathtaking good of what the Camino had to offer, made yesterday irrelevant. Today there was nothing but beauty. I loved the open trails of the Camino. Yet, there was no less beauty in small cities and towns like Burgos. This unmarked path of the Camino seemed right. And it was.

As the river stream came to an end and knowing the cathedral was somewhere near, I left the path along the river and climbed the few steps to the city streets. And there it was, just a block away – the Hotel Monjes Magnos. I was tired yet excited to be in Burgos.

I checked in, showered and napped for about three hours before going out to explore Burgos. After a quick lunch and walk along the city square, I took a tour of the Cathedral de Burgos. I then sat for a while in the huge square and enjoyed a couple glasses of wine as I watched people as they passed by. I didn't see one person I knew. Still, this was one of my favorite days on the Camino.

Before returning to the hotel, I stopped by the pharmacy for supplies. I needed surgical tape and cotton. My knee pain was no worse and fortunately I had no new blisters, but the ones I had on my heels were bigger from rubbing against the heels of my shoes. The pharmacist recommended keeping them clean and drained. She said no more Compede and to use cotton and tape to cushion the blisters from the friction caused by walking on rocks. Instead of cotton balls, I bought a package of eye make-up remover pads, tape and the suggested cream for my knee. From this day on, I used make-up pads on my feet everyday until I reached Santiago.

***** **Burgos** – *one of my favorite places on the Camino, I would love to visit it again.*

**** **Hotel Monjes Magnos** – *small but clean room, nice, friendly staff.*

Burgos to Hontanas

19.1 miles (31.5km)

I awoke early a little stiff, but rested and not too sore. There was the typical minor pain in my knee, and thankfully, no swelling. I took my sweet time getting ready. I enjoyed the solitude of having a hotel room, and at the end of the day, I would be back to albergue living, for a while at least. I wrapped my feet and toes with the newly acquired make-up pads. I was satisfied how my feet were feeling. In fact, the addition of the pad, along with the usual two pairs of socks, significantly reduced the friction against my heels. Even with the two pairs of socks during the past week, I noticed the friction had increased. I believed it had to do with weight loss. My hiking pants – the kind that zipped at the knees – were fitting loose. I had completed two full weeks and close to 200 miles (322k) on the Camino. My body was stronger and leaner. I knew I had lost weight, I hadn't expected to feel the weight loss in my feet, but my hiking shoes were now roomier.

The more distance I covered, the more I felt the need to celebrate small accomplishments. I rejoiced when I noticed increased strides, less stopping, 50 miles (80.5k), 100 miles (161.k), 200 miles (322k). They all deserved celebrating. I had an additional glass of wine, or beer at milestones. Two weeks and nearly 200 miles made me smile, and I promised myself that later I would have something special to eat or drink.

After breakfast at a café near the hotel, I started my journey at daybreak. The morning weather was fair and overcast. It was expected to be another hot day with no clouds and few trees to provide shade. In addition, about halfway to Hontanas, I would enter the Meseta. I hoped my early morning, 6:00am departure would be enough time to get me to my destination before the most intensely sunny part of the day, usually around 3:30pm.

I remembered reading about other pilgrims' experiences on the Meseta. Most dreaded it. It is barren during summer months, and because of the openness and the high elevation, the sun can be intense. During inclement weather conditions on the Meseta, pilgrims often complain of muddy paths and the lack of shelter and shade.

By the time I reached the Meseta, I was pleased with my pace, how my feet felt, and that I walked part of the way without my poles, a first. Something else to celebrate.

I had seen and spoken to several cyclists on the trail. This was the first time seeing several large groups – as many as 20 cyclists in one group.

Still, I saw no one I knew. I thought about Antonio and wondered how his father was doing. Of course, I thought about Coleen and wondered if she was still hiking or if she was now cycling. And for a moment I thought about being alone. I quickly came to the conclusion that I was doing fine. I came here alone with no expectations of growing close to anyone. I'd met people whom I cared about, but I knew this journey was mine, and all the implications (the spiritual connections, vibes, intuitions, gut) suggested that. Though people came and went, I was supposed to do this journey alone.

The pleasant weather on the Meseta held up. The skies remained partly cloudy. I walked and marveled at the continued fields of golden wheat and beautiful red poppies. I had brief conversations and exchanged pleasantries and *Buen Caminos* with fellow hikers. I met a young couple, Dave and Angie from Canada who was just starting their journey. The clean and neat clothing and shoes of a few other pilgrims indicated they were also new to the trail. Another lady, Ava, from South Africa, was doing the Camino in two-week intervals. The previous year, she did SJPdP to Burgos. This time she started in Burgos and hoped to finish in Leon and spend three days there before returning home. The following year she hoped to hike from Leon to Santiago. There were many pilgrims like Ava. They had jobs and limited time, so they hiked a few weeks each year until they completed the Camino.

Halfway to Hontunas, I wondered if I should have stopped in Hornillo since it was 6 miles (10km) closer. My feet were doing well with the makeup pads, and the relatively easy trail helped, but walking on rocks all day was taking a toll. I had plenty of water, and I stopped at every village or town to eat and drink something and to rest. I would spend 20–30 minutes at each location. Any more time would jeopardize me getting a bed now that I was on my own.

I arrived at the El Puntido Albergue in Hontunas in late afternoon tired from the long day on the trail. The make-up pads were doing the job. There were no new blisters, and after a day of constant rocks, my blisters were no worse. I had blisters on each of my big toes that were showing signs of healing. They were dry and no longer painful. There were two large blisters on each heel, and on this day, they felt better than any other time before.

After a shower and hanging my hand-washed clothes out to dry, I went downstairs to get a bocadillo and a glass of wine from the bar. I sat outside and enjoyed the sights and sounds of Hontunas.

**** ***Hontunas*** – *too tired to explore the small village, but I liked what I did see*

***** ***El Puntido Albergue*** – *a very friendly and diverse staff, great food and service, the night was cool, and I appreciated the soft, warm, comfortable blanket, another favorite*

Hontunas to Itero de la Vega

12.2 miles (19.6km)

In spite of the top bunk, I slept well. I awoke feeling good, less sore. For the second night, I was starting my hike with new pilgrims. I didn't know anyone here, and that worked for me.

Whenever I could, at least whenever WiFi allowed, I checked my phone every morning and evening. Sometimes WiFi only lasted a few hours in the evening. In most cases, it stopped around 10:00p.m. My contact with family and friends was through emails and social media, so each night I posted pictures of my day on Facebook, happy that I was able to share my journey. I was also happy that my family and dear friends knew I was safe.

Having access to my email allowed the company that transported my backpack to communication with me each day to find out my new destination. At night, after deciding my next destination, I would send the company an email letting them know. The first time I received an email from Javier at Caminofacil, I had to smile. I thought about losing touch with the people I knew, but I was happy to have gained a new friend in Javier.

It was another overcast morning. It was cool, and though most of the laundry I'd hung on the outside clothesline had dried, my socks were damp. This was one of the disadvantages when a facility didn't have a dryer.

I started the day – with my feet wrapped in make-up pads – wearing ankle socks and my hiking sandals. To help with drying my hiking socks, I pinned them to my daypack hoping they would dry soon in the likely event of rain and I needed to wear my hiking shoes.

I studied John Brierley's guide the previous night and realized there would be many elements to this day's hike. There was the beauty of Castrojeriz that I had read so much about, and I couldn't wait to see it. There was also a steep climb after Castrojeriz that I didn't look forward to. And there was the threat of rain. I left my backpack to be transported to Hogar del Peregrino in Iterro de la Vega. With the possibility of rain, I wore long hiking pants and packed my rain jacket and poncho in my daypack.

During the first week of my Camino, to pass the time on the trail, I started searching for rocks to take home as souvenirs and keepsakes to remind me of the Camino adventure. I now had about ten rocks – mostly heart shaped – in my jacket pocket. During extra-long stretches of walking through wheat fields, I would slow my stride a bit to look for something more unique to add to or replace the rocks I'd collected. It helped pass the time. It almost became an obsession. This was the leg of my journey that I found the two rocks I carried every day and brought home with me.

Leaving Hontanas, I was grateful for the flat terrain and the unforgettable beauty. There was something unique but simplistic about this area of the Camino. I came across my first souvenir vendor on the Camino. The guys with a table set-up outside of his van were selling crosses, shells, bracelets and other trinkets. I stopped and looked but didn't purchase anything. I had another three weeks to go, and I didn't want to add to my pack. After the vendor, I passed under the ancient archway of San Anton.

I stopped in the quaint village of Castrojeriz. It was yet another village where pilgrims seemed to dominate. I never saw anyone there who appeared to be a resident. Everyone was weary looking with dusty backpacks and hiking shoes as they walked throug this beautiful village. I took pictures of the beautifully crafted wooden doors with sheets of metal across the bottom. There was no one around to ask, but I assumed the metal was to protect the rich wood from weather conditions, like snow and rain.

After what seemed like an endless field of greenery and red poppies, I came upon the dreaded climb back onto the Meseta. I took a look at the mountain and tried to size up my upcoming struggle. I could only see the front side of the mountain trail, and it seemed fairly doable, nothing too strenuous. It wasn't the Pyrenees, yet I knew this wasn't going to be a quick uphill hike. I unfolded my trusted hiking poles and dug into the task at hand.

Thank goodness for the cool weather. The climb was strenuous and as good as I felt about the condition of my body and how it had adjusted to hiking everyday, I found myself back to hiking a little, then stopping to catch my breath. It was almost as bad as when I struggled over the Pyrenees. The climb was a challenge and just when I thought it was over, there was more climbing to be done on the backside of the mountain.

Once I reached the summit, I needed my rain jacket, although the soft rain and cool weather felt good. It was another proud moment to reach the summit. It was misty for the remainder of the hike.

I arrived in Itero de la Vega tired, cold, wet, and not feeling well. I wanted to take a shower and go to bed. The sweet couple that owned the Hogar del Peregrino Albergue also owned the adjacent grocery store. The albergue was a home, and I was grateful to have my own bedroom. When I checked in, I was the only one there. I wanted to go to bed, so I went to the store and ordered a bocadillo, and after dinner, I showered, and called it a night. I was asleep before nightfall, and I had no idea if any other pilgrims checked in.

***** *Itero de la Vega* – *nice, small, quaint village, easy to get in and out*

***** *Hogar de la Vega* – *having a regular bedroom with an adjacent bathroom was a treat, loved the nice couple*

Itero de la Vega to Fromista

9 miles (14.5km)

I awoke rested and feeling better. I had some congestion and a scratchy throat, but I didn't feel bad enough to stay in Itero another day. I think going to bed early helped.

With so much space in the room, I was able to take a moment and repack my backpack before sending it on to the next location. For three additional euros, the owner washed, dried, and folded my hiking clothes. Whenever laundry service was available on the Camino, I took it. 3 to 5 euros was a small price to pay to have my laundry done on occasion.

Most albergues had some kind of washing service, either a washing machine and a dryer, or a basin – usually outside – to wash your own clothes, and lines somewhere on the grounds for drying. Several times I was too tired to do laundry, and there was a time or two when no washing facility was available at all. The normal routine of the day was to come in from hiking, shower, do laundry, rest, then find something to eat and drink.

With my clothes cleaned, I repacked my backpack and daypack. Now that I was carrying only my daypack, I made sure it was always packed with essential depending on the weather. I always carried my hiking sandals and foot care products. In a small pouch, I carried medication, snacks, sunscreen, a sarong cut-in-half lengthwise that I used as a towel and as a scarf, my guidebook, mini IPAD, and extra clothing when I needed to combat cold, rain and the sun. And I carried water. My large backpack had a two-liter water container that I never used, but I was happy I brought it, just in case. I carried two store-bought bottles that I refilled while hiking.

Last night, when planning for this day's hike, I considered hiking 18 miles (30k) to Villalcazar – about 3.5 miles (6km) before Carrion. It was all flat land, and the weather was expected to be pleasant. Going all the way to Villalcazar would have shaved off a day of hiking. I was starting to worry about time and if I could complete the journey in the planned 35 days. To make it work and complete my journey in 5 weeks, I needed to average 100 miles (161k) per week. After 16 days, I had completed 190 miles (306k). I was behind and thought if I needed to make up time and distance, the Meseta would be the best place to do it. Yet I knew it would be in my best interest to slow down and allow some time for my blisters to heal. So, instead of the 18 miles (30k) to Villalcazar, I chose to do 9 miles (14.5k) to Fromista.

This was another of my favorite hiking days. As always, the views were spectacular: mountains in the distance, fields of wheat and poppies, and river streams. No matter what, I found time to stop or at least slowdown and enjoy the beauty and sounds of the running rivers.

For the first time since leaving Antonio in Burgos, I saw someone I knew. I met Noah from Brazil when I met Antonio. He was also doing the Camino solo. Noah was unforgettable because he hiked with cloth sandals; very simple, thin soles with cloth tied up his legs to just below his knees, like Roman sandals. He walked slowly, with a wooden pole. The walk was familiar, like how most pilgrims walked when they had feet or knee pain. As Noah and I walked together, he told me about the pain he was having in both ankles.

It was good to see Noah. We caught up about people we knew. He didn't know Coleen, and when I described her, he didn't remember seeing her on the trail. I told him about Antonio's sudden departure after finding out about his father falling out of bed. The only person he had seen was Sarah from Italy. The two of them had stayed at the same albergue in Burgos.

Noah and I enjoyed talking about our travels and life in our respective countries. I told him about Southern California and how I looked forward to retirement in a few years. I shared my love of travel and how I hoped to someday visit Brazil, Chile and Peru. He recommended Chile, though he thought Peru was worthy of a visit. He encouraged me to learn Portuguese before my visit.

We talked about family. Looks can be deceiving, I know, and I understand the motto *Don't judge a book by its cover*, but Noah could have been a poster-child for the word "pilgrim." He had a nomad appearance: long hair, simple clothing, wooden stick, a beard, and he said he slept only in municipal albergues and monasteries to save money. Yet during our conversation, he revealed that his highly respected parents were business owners (I didn't ask what business) and his brother, sister and brother-in-law were all lawyers. He shared how they all thought he was lazy and had no focus in his life. Taking time to walk the Camino de Santiago was stupid to them, but Noah said he had never been happier than when he was left alone to hike, explore, or do work to help others. Two years prior, he helped build homes in Africa. To him, that was the best experience in his life. He told me about meeting the love of his life in Angola. He showed me a wooden elephant he bought in Angola that reminded him of his girlfriend. I showed him my travel companion, a miniature Minnie Mouse given to me by my niece.

It was my shortest hike in a while, but it was filled with so much beauty and many fond memories. Most memorable was arriving in Fromista and seeing a group of students playing in a park. I asked them where was their teacher. I wanted to get permission to take a photo with the students. One of them responded, "Jose is over there." I got a kick out of them calling the teacher by his first name. Jose granted me permission, and I took a quick group-selfie with this beautiful, multi-cultural cluster of students. It is still one of my favorite Camino photos. And there was the moment just before arriving in town that two men were walking the Camino with a buggy filled with beautiful, sleeping newborn puppies and their mother trotting closely behind. It was a good day filled with beauty, laughter, and new life.

I arrived at the Estrella del Camino Albergue early, before they were open. I left and walked around until I found a place to stop for lunch. I had about an hour before check-in, which gave me time to take out my cell phone and look over the hundreds of pictures I had taken since leaving California as I sat enjoying a ham and queso bocadillo and a glass of wine.

An hour later, I checked into the albergue and did the usual: showered, did laundry and got about a two-hour nap before going out to further explore the town. I didn't wait until 7:00pm for a pilgrims meal; I wanted to go out and eat at one of the local cafes instead.

After I returned from eating and touring, I found a nice cozy area near the bar to relax. I sat with a glass of wine for a while and talked with a young Canadian couple. The husband was a musician, the wife a nurse. He was familiar with Southern California and the number of rappers that emerged from the area. We talked extensively about music, our favorite genres, songs, and entertainers – past and present – we had traveled to see.

Now tired, I went back to my bunk (bottom bunk, thankfully). I walked right into the middle of an argument between a man and woman. The woman, Jill, whom I'd met on the trail, had been assigned a top bunk. Instead of taking it, she moved a guy's gear and claimed the bottom bed. The man was furious when he returned, but Jill refused to move. It was the strangest situation – like a scene out of a movie. I'm sure these things happen on the Camino from time to time, but it seemed like a terrible waste of energy to take someone's assigned bunk and then argue and refuse to give it up when asked to do so. The guy ended up taking the top bunk, although he sulked for the remainder of the night.

I was resting in my bunk when I heard a discussion between Jill and another young woman. The young woman asked Jill, who had just come from a shower, if she knew there were marks on her back that looked like bedbug bites. A few people in the room confirmed that they were bedbug bites. Jill thought she might have gotten them from an albergue in the last village where she stayed the previous night. The room became alive with concerns and recommendations about how to best get rid of the bedbugs. Suggestions ranged from washing everything in the hottest water to freezing everything.

Exposure to bedbugs is one of those things pilgrims on the Camino dread most, I think more so than getting blisters. Personally, I could deal with my blisters, sore knee, and achy back. I didn't think much at all about sleeping in rooms with people who snored loudly. It was no big deal to me. If the snoring interfered with my sleep, in went my earplugs. I could function sleeping every night in a top bunk if I had to, and I could do it all without complaint.

Bedbugs were another story. Of course, I had researched all I could about bedbugs on the Camino and how best to avoid them. They were a way of life. On the

Camino, there were no guarantees that I wouldn't be exposed. All I could do was prepare.

When I purchased my sleeping bag, I also bought a recommended bedbug repellent to spray it. Three weeks before my departure from home, I began coating my sleeping bag. Overall, I coated it three times. The spray left it so smelly that I would hang it outside for days following each coating. The spray was strong with the familiar repellent smell, but I was willing to tolerate the unappealing odor to keep from contracting bedbugs.

My sleeping gear consisted of a sleeping bag that I almost always laid out over the bed. I would zip myself in whenever the weather was cool. I used my sheet set on nights when the weather was warm. I felt I had done all I could to keep from getting bitten by bedbugs. Until this day, bedbugs hadn't been an issue. Having someone in the room who clearly had bedbugs was unnerving. This was one of the many albergues I stayed where mattresses were thankfully covered in blue plastic.

Knowing a fellow pilgrim in our room had bedbug bites was certainly a mood changer. A few people – some discreetly, others not so much – moved their gear farther away from the woman's belongings.

***** *Itero de la Vega* – *loved it, plenty of cafés and small shops*

*** *Estrella del Camino* – *nice facilities, strict rules, the woman came in about 6:30am and abruptly turned on the*

*lights and opened shutters while announcing it was time
for everyone to get up*

Fromista to Carrion

12 miles (19.3km)

Needless to say, we all went to bed concerned about bedbugs, and we all woke up not very happy when the owner came in, turned on lights, and announced that we all had to get up prepare to leave. Not that I had kept track of opening and closing times of each albergue, but most had the same, or near the same, operating times. Most closed at or around 8:00am then reopened to pilgrims around 3:00pm or 4:00pm. We all vacated the premised, irritated at being rushed out.

It was another day of morning overcast and cool temperatures and welcomed flatlands. Most of the route was alongside a road. According to Brierley's guide, there was an alternative tree-shaded route, but I wasn't traveling too far, and the cloudy weather made hiking the main route bearable.

There were a few moments of chatter about the owner's actions and bedbugs, but the conversations soon gave way to the routine of the morning – overcoming stiffness, finding breakfast, and taking in the beauty of the Camino.

I walked awhile with a mother and son from Colorado. They were the third mother/child pairing I'd met. The other two were mom and daughters. As a mother of an adult daughter, I would love to have shared this adventure with her. The Camino, however, is not for everyone and knowing my daughter as I do, it definitely isn't for her. She prefers hotels and parties. Waking early every morning and putting in long days walking would not work for her.

There was such a unique beauty to each day on the Camino. Whether it was the country fields and landscape with farmland, animals, vineyards or quaint villages and towns with pretty houses decorated with fresh flowers. The Camino had many facets to it. One, the many cemeteries I saw on the trails. They were gated displays of monuments, which clearly represented how well the Spanish honored their dead. I stopped often to look at names and dates on headstones and crypts. I noticed how many of the deceased were Illuminati, a secret fraternal organization that dates back to the 1700s. Apparently, the organization has a devoted following in Spain.

It was another day of endless fields of golden wheat. About halfway through the hike, I began seeing rows and rows of beautiful yellow jasmine bushes along the trail. Even in the almost barren farmland, the jasmine was just as visually captivating as the rolling mountains of the Pyrenees, or the Rojas vineyards.

From all I had read about the Meseta, I expected complete barren land, little vegetation, and miles and miles of nothingness. Actually, I was enjoying the ease of the Meseta. I loved the beautiful mountains and accepted the challenges that came with getting up and over them. Mountains and hiking long miles every day forced me to dig deeper into myself than I ever had before. As my body became stronger, I became more confident in my ability to set and accomplish daily hiking goals.

I looked at the Meseta as a place to give pilgrims a well-deserved break. Yes, the Meseta has its challenges: heat and very few sources of shade. It is wide open with unobstructed views and fewer villages and towns. Camino rocks were always an issue for me, but I think the combination of the Meseta flatland and using the make-up pads was helping my feet heal.

I stopped in Villalcazar to take a break at the Café Bar next to the Santa Maria la Virgen Blanca Church. I wanted to go inside the church. Unfortunately, it wasn't open. I did take pictures with the statue of Santa Maria LaBlanca.

I arrived in Carrion and was surprised to see the many cafes, shops, and bars. There was a store with all the gear necessary to accommodate pilgrims on the Camino.

I decided to try something a little different this time. Instead of an albergue, I spent the night at the Santa Maria Parrish located in the town plaza. I arrived just before opening and stood in line with about twenty other pilgrims. The sweet part of checking in at the Santa Maria Parrish was the refreshments served by the nuns as we waited to register. We were treated to olives, crackers and apple juice.

The rooms were clean and comfortable, and I was happy to have a bottom bunk. I followed my routine of checking in, taking a shower, doing laundry, and then resting. The nuns announced during check-in that there would be a pilgrim sing-along during the evening. I was both excited and nervous. The idea made me smile since I was no singer by any stretch of the imagination. The only time I sing is when music is loud enough to drown out my non-singer's voice, or if I am totally alone. But singing folk songs in a Parrish was a part of the Camino I wanted to experience.

I had time before the sing-along to go out and find food. I ate a bordillos and had a glass of wine at a great little café filled with locals. It was one of my favorite places to eat. The atmosphere was alive with conversations and laughter.

I made it back to the Santa Maria Parrish and found the large gathering room filled with pilgrims waiting for the sing-along to begin. We all received a handout with lyrics to the songs. The nuns selected each song and we all followed along. It was a great evening of unexpected fun and camaraderie among pilgrims. We all ended the evening, I think, happier and less concerned about distance, foot pain or anything else. It was nice to share a happy moment with fellow pilgrims.

***** *Santa Maria* – *loved the town, great shops and cafés, a place to purchase hiking supplies, if needed*

***** *Santa Maria Parrish* – *one of my favorite experienced, loved the kindness of the nuns and the sing-along*

DAY 19

Carrion to Terradillos

16.7 miles (26.8km)

I awoke feeling good. Really good. No feet pain, my knee was holding up, and all seemed right with the Camino world. I still wondered about Coleen and thought about Antonio, but having completed half of my Camino, I now accepted the journey I was destined for. I still worried about time. Would I, could I make it to Santiago in time to catch my scheduled flight out of Madrid on July 6? The past two days had been relatively easy, but I needed to start making up time.

I got an early start. Left the nice nuns of the Santa Maria Parrish around 6:30am. I stopped for breakfast at a local café before taking to the trail. It was another good day of overcast skies and not-so-hot weather. The Brierley guide indicated another day of welcomed flatland. I was happy I had no new blisters, and the ones I had were still showing signs of healing. They were drying nicely and thanks to the foot lotion and make-up pads, other than the normal soreness from walking, there was only minimal foot pain.

It was another long day of hiking through farmland with fields of golden wheat. There wasn't much else to see, but again I enjoy the peace and solitude of it all. At the recommendation of the guidebook, I packed food and extra water since there were no villages or towns for 10 miles (17k). I also packed extra toilet paper and wipes in case nature called. My food was a bocadillos I ordered at the café the night before. I stopped at a small market before leaving Carrion and bought two bananas and two extra bottles of water. Of course, I had a package of trail mix that Antonio had given me.

The day seemed endless, more so because of the lack of rest and food stops. Like with every other day I walked the Camino, I found beauty on the trail, even in the simplest things. There were barns filled with hay and thankfully there was a small food truck in the middle of nowhere.

I spent the day walking alone. I thought about my night's stay at the Parrish and how much I enjoyed it. I believe in God, I pray, and I try to live a life of righteousness by giving back and helping others. On the Camino when I went into the beautiful churches and cathedrals, I would pray and give thanks for all I have, for this opportunity, and for the safe journey of all the pilgrims.

The time I was spending alone allowed me to reconnect with my spiritual self. I had no need to listen to music on the Camino since the sights and sounds of nature, and occasional silence allowed me to breathe deeply and just be. Staying at the Santa Maria Parrish allowed me to experience the Catholic faith that is so much a part of the Camino. My heart was still filled with joy from the simple pleasure of singing along with the nuns and fellow pilgrims.

Halfway through the hike, I walked upon this narrow path that was surrounded by bush after bush of yellow jasmine. It was the second day that I was able to take in the beauty of the yellow blooms.

I stopped in Calzadilla, the only town between Carrio and Terradillos for a cool drink. The town was next to a road, and when I left, I saw a sign just ahead indicating an alternate route. Not thinking twice, I choose the alternative route.

I crossed onto a graveled road toward the fields of wheat. Not only did I walk 6 miles of fields, but this part was also different because this route crossed directly onto farmlands, closer to homes and barns and workers. Worse yet, I didn't remember seeing one yellow arrow or sign indicating I was on the right path, and I thought for a moment that maybe I wasn't. I never was too concerned since I walked parallel to the main path. I didn't know if I had taken a wrong turn or not, but I was on this road alone. I never saw anyone else, not even a farmer to ask if I was headed in the right direction. At one moment I stopped and took out the guide to look at the map.

Although there were times I found the guide complicated and unclear; I had reached a point when I understood – most of the time – distance and directions based on the map. I could determine the intended path by reading signs on the Camino. They were always well marked, but there were those occasions when painted yellow arrows or markers were obstructed by trees or overgrown bushes. The few times I questioned which direction I should go, I found that stopping and thoroughly looking around, often solved the problem.

Covering 16.7 miles (27km) would take me well into the afternoon. After the Zubiri descent on day two, I was averaging about three miles an hour of straight walking. Stopping for rest and food breaks added time. The 16.7 miles (27km) to Terradillos would take 6 to 7 hours on this fairly warm day.

One reason why I didn't hesitate taking this route was again because of the Brierley guide. The little green dots on the map indicating the alternate path led right to the albergue I had chosen, and sure enough, after the six miles of nothing but wheat fields and no other pilgrim, the path thankfully ended right in front of the Jacques de Molay Albergue.

I was tired from the intense afternoon sun. I checked in, and when the lady walked me up to my room, she had placed me in a small corner room with four beds (no bunks). Three of the beds were occupied by men. She looked at me and I at her. I think she understood that I would've had a problem with this arrangement. She said, "No, no. Come with me." She led me to a room down the hall with only two beds, one occupied by Kary from Germany. I had seen her many times before and we had talked on occasion. She began the Camino alone, but recently she was traveling with a guy.

After I went downstairs and had dinner, I returned, and she and I talked about our Camino journey. This was her second. The Camino was a way of life for Kary and many other Europeans. It was nothing for a group of friends or family members to come together and walk all or part of the Camino. It is no big deal either to do it solo. The guy I'd seen Kary with was someone she had met in Burgos. He started with his friends, but after meeting her, he started waiting around to walk with her. At first, she was good with it, but she was missing the time alone. She knew that she needed to come up with a way to tell him, hoping he would be OK and move along.

Kary and I spent the evening talking. The conversation flowed easily until we could no longer stay awake. It was another day to be grateful for the little things: safety, the small room with only two beds, and a good end-of-the-evening conversation.

*****Terradillos* – *came into the village from the backside, so I didn't see much of it*

***** *Jacques de Molay Albergue* – *another favorite, great food, wonderful staff, clean, everyone raved about the hamburgers*

Terradillos to Calzadilla

14.6 miles (23.5km)

This was another day of welcomed flatland and no hills or mountains. My blisters were still healing, and my knee was stiff as usual, but not sore. To get through the days, I was still taking the normal dosage of 800mg of ibuprofen each morning after breakfast.

I started the day early, around 7:00am, to clear skies. Before hitting the trail, I sat down and studied the Brierley guide one more time. Following Antonio's printout of places he would have stayed, I needed to be sure I followed the correct route to get me to Calzadilla de los Hermanillos. Luckily, I did stop and review it. Calzadillos is only accessible by way of the alternative route (Via Romana). Missing the turnoff would have been a problem. Going out of my way would have meant turning back or taking a taxi to get to the albergue in Calzadillos where my backpack had been sent. At the start of the day, I knew I needed to keep a keen watch for the turnoff at Calzada del Coto.

It was a nice beginning to the day. I was happy to know that four villages existed along the day's trail. After yesterday's long stretch of walking with only two stopping points, it was good to know that there would be ample rest and food stops for the reminder of my days on the Camino.

The day warmed quickly. Before leaving the albergue I applied a liberal amount of my recently purchased 50spf sunscreen in preparation for the heat. I was at least three-shades darker and I was still doing all I could to keep the back of my neck from getting sunburned. So far no burn, but the daily exposure to the intense sun had me worried.

I was now in the Castilla Y Leon (Leon) region of Spain. Exhausted from the heat, I was happy to reach the town of Sahagun, about 8 miles (13k) beyond Terradillos. It was another special place on the Camino. Most striking were the arena and the yellow and white structure at the town's entrance. There were adult storks perched high atop buildings guarding eggs and younglings against flying prey.

I took a much-needed rest and had lunch with Kary from Germany. She and I were taking different routes. She was going on to Bercianos del Real Camino. I liked talking with her, and I hoped I would see her again.

I passed the River Cea and knew I was only a short distance from the turnoff that would put me on the route to Calzadillos de las Hermanillos. I saw six other pilgrims on the road just before the turnoff onto the alternative route. Only one of them turned off with me. It was an Asian woman about my age who I hadn't seen before. She had a fast pace. By the time I passed the village of Calzada del Coto, she was far ahead of me. I had her in my sight for about a mile, but then she was gone.

This was my *fussiest* day on the Camino. I was irritated and in a crappy mood. I didn't like the route, and there was no way of escaping it. The graveled road – with no source of shade – continued right through farmland with barns and buildings packed with hay, animals and farming equipment. I was alone, and at one point I came upon a group of men working in and around one of the many barns. It wasn't the ideal situation. I wasn't going to chance my safety if I could help it, so I reached into my fanny pack and took out the Swiss Army knife I'd bought in Roncesvalles (Day 2). Just in case. I smiled, responded to their greetings and kept moving.

I'm a product of the inner city of Chicago, Illinois. What I learned while trying to survive those often-mean streets was to stay aware of my surroundings. I didn't have a problem with looking back over my shoulder then or on the Camino to make sure I wasn't being followed. Looking behind me is something I did regularly on the Camino, from day one. I walked alone most of the time, and I was never comfortable with anyone walking behind me. It was nothing for me to slow down or stop altogether and allow people to pass me. Thankfully, it all went well. I passed the area, and the men were soon out of my sight.

It was hot and there was no shade. With about 2 miles (3.2k) to go, I stopped to rest and hydrate. I had just enough water for me to make it to my destination. What made me exasperated was Brierley's guide.

Up to this point, I'd had no problem with Brierley's description of places or his maps. Brierley's descriptions provided significant details about routes, distances, and information about each destination, but there were no details about this route. He referred to this as "the alternative scenic route (less travelled, but little shade)." Bad choice of words. Just to be clear, my intention is to point out that someone could have a medical emergency on this "less travelled, but little shade" route, and it could spell trouble for anyone out there all alone.

I never once thought about what the town of Calzadilla de los Hermanillos or the albergue would be like. The small village appeared liked a welcomed oasis. The Via Trajana Albergue, the first albergue off the trail, was an even better sight.

After a routine check-in, I forced my tired body up the three flights of stairs to one of the nicest rooms I'd had on the Camino. There were four single beds with nice clean sheets and warm blankets. It was one of those special moments on the Camino when I didn't need a sleeping bag or my sheet set. I showered a little longer just to cool my body down. After finishing my laundry, I went in search of food. I was hungry and very thirsty. I knew from my research that most places on the Camino didn't offer ice. I prefer room temperature water, so I never asked. Whenever I wanted something cold, I ordered a bottle of Nestle Ice Tea or a beer. This time I wanted something icy cold. I ordered two bottles of water and two cold beers.

The alternative route apparently wasn't very popular. I sat on the patio of the café and watched as a few pilgrims entered Calzadilla de los Hermanillos. Maybe the village was too new to the Camino, or maybe it was too far off the main path.

I returned to my room and saw the lady who had passed me on the trail. She shared that her Camino started in Burgos. Walking the Camino was her dream come true. I listened to her story as she sat on the bed nursing her first blister.

Later, while reflecting on the day, I thought about how my Camino adventure had changed since Burgos. I still hadn't seen Coleen or talked to anyone who had seen her. Antonio was back home in Puerto Rico caring for his father who hopefully was doing well. The Camino trails were now flatter, at a higher elevation. Since I was still using Antonio's guide sheet for albergues I thought the company he had used was probably working with less populated, new places on the Camino, especially here in the flatter regions. I loved these off locations, the quiet nights and the solitude, but I wondered if it was the reason I wasn't seeing Coleen and other pilgrims I started with.

I thought about the challenge of the day's hike, the heat, and being alone and hesitant when I saw the group of men. I thought about how good I felt overall. I was here doing something that challenged me mentally, physically, and emotionally. I was proud, period. I tallied my mileage, and in 20 days I had completed 255 miles (410km), over halfway to Santiago. I still had long ways to go, but I had come far.

I was feeling accomplished by stepping out of my comfort zone to get here, to do this. I accepted whatever challenge I would face from here to Santiago, and for now, I was good.

The Longest Day – I stayed up awhile and wrote. At one point I looked out the window at the setting sun at 10:15pm. I checked Facebook and discovered it was the Longest Day.

***** ***Calzadilla de los Hermanillos*** *– nice small village, the challenge was on the trail getting there*

***** ***Via Trajana Albergue*** *– great staff, newer facility, comfortable bed, nice décor*

Calzadilla to Raliegos

12.7 miles (20.5km)

I awoke early to the sound of my roommate packing. Grateful for the good night's sleep, I stayed in bed until well after she left, then took my sweet time getting myself ready for the day's hike. I felt good. No pain, only the usual muscle soreness. I had enough eye make-up pads for my feet to last another week or so, but I needed to purchase surgical tape the first chance I got. I didn't want to run out. I had replenished my two water bottles and packed two bags of trail mix, courtesy of Antonio. I carried my backpack downstairs for pick up and was ready to begin my day on the trail.

The sky was blue and clear for miles. I studied the guide last night – no longer upset with John Brierley. My mini-tantrum forgotten. I hit the trail early and had to stop almost immediately and take pictures of the breathtaking sunrise. The trail was more of the usual fields of golden wheat and the occasional farmhouse, but the views were stunning. I appreciated the simplicity of the Camino's golden land and endless blue skies.

Choosing the alternative route and staying in Calzadilla had its advantages. I had a shorter walk today because I was closer to my next destination, Raliegos. It was definitely a day when food and water were needed on the trail. This morning I awoke filled with gratitude that I'd made the decision to transport my backpack and carried only a simple, lightweight daypack. I wore my knee brace from day one, and thankfully, I wasn't having knee pain. The brace was a benefit, but I knew not carrying the twelve-pound backpack was the reason for the absence of pain.

This was yet another day that I wished for a hiking hat to cover the back of my neck. Using sunscreen and covering my neck with the sarong helped, but the sun on my back was intense. The path was covered with large and small rocks, and about halfway to Reliegos, I started to feel the irritating rubbing on my feet that came from stepping on rocks.

I thought about what I had learned while researching this area. Apparently, people have a love-hate relationship with this section of the Camino. The section between Burgos and Leon is primarily flat with little to see beyond farmland and rivers. It could be hot, and there are long stretches from one village to the next. Those who loved it – like I did – enjoyed time to themselves and accepted that the Meseta was a part of the Camino. Then, there were people who didn't like it and would try to avoid it or move past the area as quickly as they could. Many pilgrims did so by taking the bus or putting in longer days to hike the extra miles. This is the perfect area to make up time, if needed. There are 119 miles (180k) from Burgos to Leon. It was not impossible for me to cover the distance in four or five days. In retrospect, this was where I probably should have put in more miles each day to lessen my worry about reaching Santiago in time to fly home on July 6. The flatland was good for me. My blisters were healing, and I was comfortable with my pace. By the end of each day, my feet were sore and tired and adding three to five mile each day would have possibly increased the chance of aggravating the blisters or developing new ones. Still, I had just passed the half way mark on Day 20 of my journey, and I had fifteen days to complete the second half. With blisters healing, I hoped to start making up time.

I arrived in Reliegos happy I'd chosen to do 11 miles (19km) instead of more. It was hot, and I was tired. My pace was quicker and put me in Reliegos before the albergue had opened, and those occasions for me were very rare. I found a nearby café and stopped for food, water, and a Nestles Ice Tea. I found an outside table where I sat and watched pilgrims and residents pass by. Although each town shared common cultural and religious practices, each had its own rhythm and style. Today I watched two children, one a boy who looked to be about 11 or 12, and a younger girl about 6 or 7. They may have been brother and sister. It made me smile to watch the boy teaching the girl to ride a bike. He was so patience with her. It was a beautiful, precious sight that fit right in with what the Camino represented...the simple pleasures of life.

141

I walked the short distance down the road and around the corner from the café to the LaParada Albergue. I checked in, showered, hand-washed and hung my laundry in the outdoor common area. I ordered a glass of wine and sat on the patio with my feet up. I was soon joined by Diane and Joe from Texas. They had that now-familiar fresh and rested look. They were energetic and had no deep tan lines from sun exposure, and no stiff walk, all common indicators of people new to the Camino.

Diane and Joe began their journey in Burgos. They had dreamed of doing the Camino for the past few years. Health issues derailed their original plan to do the entire Camino so they decided to do what they could. Their plan was to walk some, bus, and take the train here and there, all within three weeks' time.

We talked for a while, sharing wine and stories. As the evening set in, Diane suggested cooking dinner together instead of eating at a restaurant. I never had the slightest notion about cooking on the Camino, even when I saw other people doing it. Cooking in albergues was common when kitchens were available. The benefit was it created an opportunity to prepare and share a meal with fellow pilgrims. It was also cost-effective. Albergues provided pilgrim meals from 9 to 15 euros. The meals varied. Most came with salad, soup and a main dish of beef or chicken, potatoes, dessert, and all the wine you could drink – within reason, of course. 5 or 6 people sharing the expense of cooking a meal could eat for half the total cost of a pilgrims meal.

I shared pilgrim meals a few times on the Camino. They were served at 7:00pm, but I didn't like eating that late. The few times I did eat them, it was to enjoy the company of fellow pilgrims.

Cooking in albergues also meant cleaning. You cook, you clean. There were no maid services to clean for you. I didn't want to clean. Diane convinced me to join her in cooking and cleaning. I decided to go with it and chalk it up as another Camino experience.

Diane, Joe and I took a short break before meeting outside after inquiring about the location of the grocery store. Diane's husband wasn't any help with menu planning. He just wanted to make sure we had wine. We found the grocery store that was small, but efficient. It had nothing extra, only the basics, but we found everything needed for our pasta dish.

Diane did most of the cooking. Joe and I cleaned. We sat and talked about our travels and the places we'd like to visit next. We said our goodbyes, well-wishes and Buen Caminos. This would be the only time I would see Diane and Joe.

**** *Reliegos* – *quaint, with a nice shady village square*

**** *La Parada Albergue* – *friendly staff, great patio, nice addition of vending machines with snacks, water, and coffee*

Reliegos to Leon

15 miles (25km)

I awoke excited. My next destination was Leon, the largest city on the Camino. Prior to researching the Camino, I had heard of only two places: Pamplona and Leon. Leon would give a momentary break from the solitude I had enjoyed since leaving Burgos.

I packed for the day, adding extra water in preparation for the forecasted heat. I chose to wear my sandals to begin the day, with my hiking shoes in my daypack, just in case. I had breakfast at the café where I'd eaten the day before. After a croissant, café con leche, orange juice and half an ibuprofen, I was ready to begin my journey to Leon. There would be only one trail after Mansilla, which was about 4 miles (6.5k) from Reliegos. No more alternative routes. There was a gradual incline of about 100 meters, but overall the land was flat.

On the main route, I saw Tom from Canada and Jai from Japan. I enjoyed the week on my own, but seeing familiar faces was like seeing dear friends. I inquired about

Coleen and a few other people that the three of us knew. Jai had walked a couple of days with Coleen. Coleen, she said, had wondered about me as well. She mentioned that Coleen was also hopeful the two of us would reunite sometime soon before our Camino journeys ended. I envisioned the two us meeting and sharing stories about our respective journeys since we separated in Santa Domingo on Day 11. I assumed she knew about Antonio's departure, but I wanted to share my version of what happened. I wanted to share the tale of leaving my shoes and the adventure of getting them back. I wanted to know how she was doing, who had she seen. And most of all, I wanted to know her last name, address and telephone number to ensure further contact. I wanted her to know that I missed her company and, selfishly, I missed having someone to check in with each day. There were so many stories on the Camino, and I wanted to share mine with the person I'd started this journey with. My conversation with Jai gave me hope that soon Coleen and I would reconnect.

I had the feeling that Tom and Jai were equally happy to see another familiar face. The three of us surmised that in general, the people you start the Camino with might not necessarily be the people you are with at the end of the journey. Paces are different, new friendships, acquaintances, and love interests are established, and people move on.

The three of us stopped in Arcahueja for lunch. Jai decided to take the bus to Leon. She had a noticeable limb that became more pronounced as we walked. Tom and I understood and wished her well. He and I walked together for a while, but after stopping in Puento Castro, he picked up his pace and was soon gone.

Arriving into Leon amidst all the traffic and people and the sights and noise, was a welcomed contrast from the many days of solitude, rural and the quiet. During my days since leaving Burgos, my eyes would take in the incredible views of distant mountains and skies that went on forever. But here, there was so much more to see, tall buildings, traffic, people, lots of people in motion. There were cafés, parks, shops, clothing stores and familiar American-size hotels, and the sounds of them all.

I had no idea where I was going, but I followed embedded shells in the walkways because that's what I knew to do. I walked into what I thought was the heart of the city and decided I would never find the Albergue San Francisco de Asis without directions. I flagged a passing taxi, and when he told me I was about three blocks away, I hopped in for the short ride.

The Albergue San Francisco de Asis was unique from all the other albergues I'd experienced. It was more like a hotel with its multiple levels and security camera at the sign-in desk. It was all business with the guys at the reception area. Rules were given – a first – about what time pilgrims needed to be in. Everyone needed to be in by 10:00pm. No exceptions. I wasn't sure if other albergues had curfew rules. It was never brought up, never explained before.

I was assigned to a room with two young women from China who appeared to be in their early twenties. I was given a lower bunk, thankfully. A third young woman joined us later that afternoon. She was French and was assigned to the bunk above me. We all settled in, showered and dressed, ready to go out and enjoy the sights of Leon.

The first thing I wanted was food. I ate at a café that provided the perfect view of the beautiful cathedral. I sat for a while, enjoying my meal as I watched people pass by, some obviously pilgrims by the way they were dressed. About an hour later, I took the pilgrims tour of the cathedral before walking around Leon. There was an apparent cultural fair going on in the city center. I sat again and enjoyed the beautiful celebration and the livelihood of Leon. It was a beautiful evening.

I returned to my room in the early evening. The young ladies from China were still out, but I found the room occupied by the French girl and three males, who I assumed were her friends. The men were all stretched out on the other girls' bunks. I know about five French words, so I had no idea what they were discussing when I walked in. I wasn't comfortable with them being there, and I'm sure my stern, who-are-you-and-what-are-you-doing-here expression made that clear.

I was tired, and I wanted nothing more than to lie in my bunk, write in my journal and take a nap, but I was too annoyed with the presence of the men who obviously were not assigned to the room, and probably were not guests of the albergue. I sat in the one chair of the room with my cold, sheer look of annoyance. I tried to make them feel as uncomfortable as I felt. This wasn't their room. They were intruding, and I wanted them gone. The French girl finally had had enough of me, and whatever she said to the men, they got up, clearly unhappy, grabbed their backpacks and left. The three girls came back about an hour later, and all was well again. I let the incident pass without saying a word.

The livelihood and rhythm of Leon lasted through the night. I slept by an opened window, and all night there were people walking, talking and having a good time as they passed by. I assumed it was a favorite party spot for locals and young pilgrims. As a tourist visiting Spain, Leon is as much a favorite place to visit as Madrid and Barcelona.

***** **Leon** – *beautiful, touristy city, it was nice seeing people other than pilgrims*

** **Albergue San Francisco de Asis** – *unclean, no sheets, dark, no food service, my second least favorite albergue*

PART III

The Beginning
of the End

Leon to San Martin del Camino

15 miles (25km)

I awoke early, around 5:30am, ready to leave the albergue. With the exception of the San Francisco de Asis Albergue, I enjoyed Leon. Its beauty, culture, and liveliness made it unforgettable.

After having my usual breakfast at a nearby café, I was ready to begin my journey to San Martin, but first I had to walk through Leon, a city just as interesting leaving as when I arrived. Leon is a large city. It's impossible to see it all in one day. The route back to the Camino trail made it possible for pilgrims to experience more of the city. I went slow, took my time and enjoyed more statues, parks, and beautiful architectural structures and monuments.

It was a long walk getting out of Leon. I was surprised to see more storks perched atop buildings within the city limits. I didn't see any familiar faces, yet it felt good to get back to the quiet of the trail. I began to think about my time and experience in Europe.

This was my second trip to Spain. Before, it was a part of a 10-day European trip with friends and fellow jazz lovers. Our destination was the North Seas Jazz Festival in Rotterdam, Netherlands. We also visited Barcelona, Paris, Prague, and Amsterdam. My favorite place was Barcelona. It was the food, the people, the culture, and architecture that won me over. I found Pamplona, Burgos, and Leon fascinating for the same reasons, although each city came with its own unique flavor and rhythm.

There were few places to stop along this route. It was a hot day, so I did stop in La Virgen for an iced tea. The main route kept me close to the highway, where only an occasional car or small truck passed. My destination was San Martin, about 4 miles (6.4km) beyond Villadangos. Just before San Martin, I saw a yellow arrow with the distance to Santiago listed below it. 298km (185 miles). Another milestone. 300 miles (483km) under my belt. This was Day 23, 3 weeks down and 2 weeks to go (hopefully). It made me smile. I felt accomplished and less apprehensive about my remaining time. My blisters were healing nicely, and there were no new ones. My pace was good. I took fewer fatigue breaks. Without injury and sickness, I was confident I would arrive into Santiago by Day 35.

I stopped for water and food, and at times, to get relief from the blaring sun. Just before San Martin, there was a tree-lined path that offered welcomed shade and more incredible beauty. The trees were filled little furry white cotton balls, and with the presence of the slight breezed, the blooms floated throughout the air, looking like snow. There were small mounds of the blooms on the sides of the trail, adding to the appearance of a snowy trail. It was eerie and beautiful.

I arrived into San Martin and realized that my albergue was the last one in the village. After a long walk under the intense sun, it felt like I would never make it. From studying the Brierley guide, I had learned how to read the locations of albergues in Camino villages and towns. The first albergue was listed as (1), the second as (2), and so on. I was staying at the San Martin Municipal Albergue, (4), the last one in town. The benefit to staying at the end of town was being closer to the trail when leaving the following day. The downside, a longer walk through town after a long, tiring day of hiking.

Check-in done, I was given a room with eight bunks. The mother and son from Colorado were there along with Tom from Canada. The albergue had a nice shady yard with a few tables and chairs, perfect for relaxing. There was also a basin and clothesline for doing laundry. I washed my hiking clothes and bought a cold beer and sat at one of the tables with my feet up. During my 23 days on the Camino, I had done only a few pilgrim meals. I decided to share one on this day. At the beginning of the Camino, pilgrim meals are normally shared since many pilgrims are excited and curious about other pilgrims and the journey that lies ahead. As time passing, I noticed the gatherings for pilgrim meals had become smaller.

I stayed out in the yard until the 7:00pm meal. I needed to do all I could to stay awake until mealtime. Long hiking day, especially on hot days, still made me tired, and once I made it to my destination, usually around 3:00pm or 4:00pm, I still wanted to shower, do my laundry, find food, and relax. Most nights, by 7:00pm I was relaxing – usually in my bunk.

I joined 6 other pilgrims in the dining area. None of them were people I knew or had seen before. Four were new to the Camino, two started in Burgos, two just starting in Leon. The couple from Leon had had a tough first day. The wife had intense knee pain that she thought was caused by her heavy backpack. The three of us who started in SJPdP recommended lightening her pack or having it transported until she felt better.

It was nice to sit and engage in good conversation. The young couple that started in Burgos were from Great Britain. We shared stories about the current political climates of our respective homelands. Both of our countries were experiencing upcoming elections that would bring major changes to our respective homelands.

I love food, and consider myself a 'foodie.' I like to cook. My favorite television shows are food shows. In spite of the pain that went along with walking long hours everyday, it was a special treat to be able to eat good food. I had completed three weeks on the Camino, and I didn't need a scale to know I had lost weight. Three weeks ago, my light blue jacket wouldn't zip around the fanny pack I wore around my waist, but now, the jacket zipped over the trail just fine and was loose overall. My black hiking pants were roomier as well. I hadn't been overeating. There had been days when I had to force myself to eat because I needed food for energy.

My love for the foods of Spain was no different on this day. For the fourth time, I ate Paella. This was the best of all.

The evening ended with good company and the joy of making new acquaintances.

**** *San Martin* – *very small village, not very much to see or do*

***** *San Martin Municipal Albergue* – *nice facility, great staff, comfortable beds, excellent food and service, loved it*

San Martin to Astorga

16 miles (26km)

I left San Martin at 7:15am headed to Astorga, a small city on the Camino that I looked forward to seeing. It was a beautiful, clear day with the usual forecasted heat. I still felt good. My blisters were healing and still, no new ones. The knee pain was minimized with the daily dose of ibuprofen. The morning stiffness was there, as always, but eased up after the first couple of miles on the trail. Once everything loosened and the pain numbed, normal walking – as normal as could be expected under the circumstances – resumed.

I hiked on the main route, happy to see a few people I knew. The mother and son from Colorado walked just ahead of me. The sister and brother from Georgia were also on the trail. We all looked a bit weary of our travels, yet stronger. New pilgrims were easy to spot. They didn't look as worn, and their gear still clean.

I washed my hair each time, but because I wore a cap everyday, there were times when I would run my fingers through my hair and not comb it. I wore my hair short and I wore a headband to bed, so taking time to comb my hair was never a priority. I looked weather-beaten from the constant exposure to the sun. My legs below my knees were shades darker than above the knee, and my face, arms, and neck had their own color hue going on. The 50spf sunscreen helped, but I still had a variety of color hues going on. Pilgrims new to the Camino didn't look over-tanned, and their hair was still in presentable styles.

There was a bridge just before the entry into Hospital de Orbigo. A few pilgrims were there taking pictures. The brother and sister from Georgia and I stopped for a while, took pictures and talked about the Camino. I immediately asked about Coleen, but neither had seen her.

The brother was in obvious pain. He tried to put a positive spin on his achy feet and said repeatedly that he was fine. His sister said otherwise. For the past two nights, she had pleaded with him to take a day off or take a bus to the next town. When he kept saying no, she suggested he ship his backpack for a couple of days to give his blisters a chance to heal. He rejected all her suggestions.

I stood on the bridge with them laughing as she proceeded to rant about him being unreasonable and stubborn. Their plan was to arrive in Sarria by a certain day and join two sisters who were flying in from Atlanta to join them for the last 75 miles (121km) to Santiago. He was pushing to make it to Sarria, but he still had over 100 miles (170km) to go.

Getting back on the main route proved to be effective for reconnecting with a few pilgrims I knew. The young Camino Couple – as they had come to be known – were still together. John was from Hong Kong, but his family moved to Canada when he was five. Ami lived in Hong Kong. John began the Camino with three friends but soon abandoned them to walk with Ami.

They walked hand in hand, and at one point, I saw John take Ami's backpack from her and carry it, along with his own. He carried his on his back and hers across his chest. I saw John at the Jacques de Molay Albergue in Terradillos waiting for Ami to come down for dinner.

During our conversation, he told me about his life in Canada. As a medical student, he was trying to figure out how to complete his studies and work on having a life with Ami. He had fallen hard for Ami. To him, she was 'the one.' When Ami came down, I asked her about her family and how they felt about their 19-year-old daughter hiking the Camino alone. I was a little shocked when she told me that her parents actually encouraged her to take the trip.

The Camino de Santiago is apparently quite popular in Hong Kong, and parents readily send their teenage and young adult children to experience the adventure of the Camino. There were quite a few young Asian girls on the Camino, some hiking solo, others with one or two partners.

I wondered when my daughter was young would I have encouraged her to spend 30-plus days hiking alone in another country. I'd like to think I would, but I'm not sure.

I saw another familiar person. Dave from Canada hiked alone. He kept to himself most of the time. He talked very little and never during the times I saw him did he smile. One time I struck up a conversation with him. I told about my life, where I lived and worked. He shared nothing except that he was from Canada. He asked about my backpack. I told him I was having it transported to take some of the weight off my arthritic knee and to keep my blisters from getting worse.

I knew talking to Dave was a mistake when he told me that a Camino isn't legitimate if a person doesn't walk it, in its entirety, with a full backpack. At that point, I needed to end the conversation quickly, but not before telling him what I thought about his declaration. I tried to deliver my response as sensibly and tactfully as I could without having my tone betray how I really felt. I let him know that I thought he was being judgmental. I told him that the beauty of the journey was for people to experience the Camino however they chose. He was quiet and from that point on, we only acknowledged each other with a brief smile or nod when we crossed paths.

I slowed down to walk alone as it returned to farmland. I watched endless skies, cattle feedings, and saw houses surrounded by beautiful flowers. At the highest point on the trail, there was a viewpoint with a stone cross in the middle, a few benches and a picnic table. It was a nice place to sit, enjoy a snack, and rest my tired feet. It was so beautiful; I wanted to stay longer, but I still had some distance to travel, though seeing Astorga off in the distance made the remaining time seem shorter.

This was my 24th day on the Camino and nothing I had seen before this moment had shocked me. Every trail, village, town, city, and region was unique, but nothing was unusual or out of place, not until this day.

I wasn't prepared for the green monster bridge just before the climb into Astorga. Talk about out of place. The green, modern, metal monstrosity was like nothing I had seen on the Camino. It was too modern for a place that has been around for centuries. The appearance was one thing, but the back and forth design was beyond unusual.

It had been a long day and I was tired by the time I reached the green bridge. The up and down, back and forward trek over the bridge as it crossed over a simple railroad added more distance to the journey. I was glad to be up and over it.

I was now in the Astorga city limits and before reaching my destination, I had to maneuver the steep hill and the city center to get to the San Javier Albergue. I loved walking through each location's city center or village/town square. Astorga's city center reminded me of Pamplona: the shape of it, the restaurants, the many shops, and the lively people. I decided that after I showered and rested, I would walk back to the center and find food.

It had been a long hot day on the trail, and I was tired and dusty. It was one of those days that I longed for a long hot bath, but I had to be OK with a hot shower. I was assigned to a room with four bunks and two single beds. Thankfully, I was given one of the singles.

Showered and laundry done, I wanted to get out and tour Astorga. The hostel was only a short distance from the cathedral so I decided to take a tour. There was always a special price for pilgrims wanting to tour cathedrals. I later found a restaurant in the city center where I enjoyed pizza, ice tea, water and a glass of wine.

I returned to the hostel by early evening, made myself comfortable in the common area, wrote in my journal and posted on Facebook to let everyone know I was fine.

This was my first associated hostel, a facility – according to Brierley's guidebook – "owned and run by local Spanish or other national confraternities, sometimes in conjunctional with the local authority." They tend to be cheaper than the private albergues I generally preferred. Hostels cost around 7 euros and private albergues between 9 and 12 euros.

While lying in bed, I talked with two friends from South Africa who started in Leon. This was their third year walking the Camino. They both were nurses and weren't able to take more than two weeks off at a time. Since Burgos, most of the new people I'd met were doing the Camino in segments for one reason or another, but usually because of jobs restrictions or family obligations. I realized most people who began their Camino in SJPdP were either retired or students on summer break.

***** **Astorga** – *small city, great restaurants and shops, beautiful cathedral*

**** ***San Javier Assoc Hostel*** – *friendly staff, nice facility, old building*

Astorga to Foncebadon

15 miles (25km)

I was up and out of the hostel by 6:30am. Last night, I made the decision to hike an additional 3 miles (5km) to Foncebadon. Instead of stopping in Rabanal 12.8 miles (20.6km), I decided to get some much-needed extra mileage in. After Rabanal was a steady uphill climb to Cruz de Ferro, the highest point on the Camino. While the Pyrenees peaked at 4757 feet (1450m), Cruz de Ferro did so at 4970 feet (1515m). I looked forward to seeing the monument, but I knew tackling the climb all in one day would be a challenge.

I was grateful for the mostly-flatland since Itero (Day 18). My feet were better - still healing with no new blisters. My knee didn't hurt as much, and my body continued to get stronger. I knew more mountains were to come and I felt good about my ability to handle them. Going to Foncebadon would put me in the mountains, only a short distance from Cruz de Ferro. It was a good decision.

I stopped in a beautiful chapel on my way out of Astorga, left a donation and said a prayer for the safe travel of all pilgrims. I walked with a few people I knew: the mother and son from Colorado, Arturo from Puerto Rico, and Tom from Canada. It was a nice overcast morning, and it would be a long day on the trail.

Like everyday, I needed breakfast, a café con leche, and ibuprofen to prepare my body and mine for the day's hike. I was always happy to have three or four villages to stop if necessary for food or rest before reaching my destination. I liked having time to relax, hydrate and eat something. Today there would be four village options: Murias de Rechivalda, Santa Catalina, Ganso, and Rabanal.

During the late night in Astorga, I thought seriously about my remaining time on the Camino. I had eleven days to make it to Santiago before my scheduled flight from Amsterdam to Los Angeles. I hesitated to book the Santiago flight not knowing when I would arrive. I was concerned. I could be delayed for any reason: weather, fatigue, injury. I had a 6:00am flight out of Amsterdam on July 6, and I was cutting it close.

I imagined that I wasn't the first person on the Camino to have concerns about making it to Santiago in time to make a scheduled return flight. I didn't know how much it would cost to change my flight, but I knew if I had to, it would be costly.

I had completed 316 miles (508km), with 184 miles (296km) left to Santiago. It meant walking farther each day. In the chapel at the start of the day's hike, I also prayed for the strength to finish this journey.

Prior to this day, I had seen a few tributes and monuments to the deceased. Today, there were more than ever. There were crosses and written poems saluting loved ones. There were pictures of women and men, some hiking the Camino. Along one fenced area, there were handmade wooden crosses. I wondered if they had been made by landowners or by pilgrims. All the villages were fairly small, and the residents I saw were elderly adults. I imagined small villages and towns, like Murias de Rechivalda, Santa Catalina and Sansa with very few residents, depended largely on pilgrims to provide revenue.

I stopped in each village for a restroom break, refreshments, or to relax for a while. In the last village of Rabanal del Camino, I stopped for about 45 minutes, had a bocadillos and a café con leche to prepare for the last 3 miles (5km) trek up the mountain to Foncebadon.

Most people I walked with decided to stay in Rabanal. I left Rabanal alone, and I briefly wondered if I had taken on too much. This was one of the few days that, if I were carrying my backpack, I would have stayed in Rabanal with the rest of the people I walked with. Tired as I was, I had to go on to meet up with my backpack.

The climb was not too tough. It was just a normal Camino climb with rocks and small boulders. Because I was stronger and more confident, I took it in stride and endured the added 3 miles (5km) stretch. In the end, I was glad I did because the extra distance would put me closer to the Cruz de Ferro the following day.

Foncebadon was a small village of abandoned wooden buildings and few residents. It also had a breathtaking mountain view. I checked into the LaPosada de Druid Albergue and was greeted by the very friendly mother and daughter owners. I was assigned an upper bunk in a room with four bunks. I didn't mine. I loved this place. The friendliness of the owners and the incredible views from the mountain, made me grateful for this incredible journey. After a shower and I had finished my laundry, I heard music coming from nearby. I purchased a ham and queso bocadillo and a glass of wine and went out to find the source.

Outside, at one of the albergues across the road was a group of pilgrims, some dancing, others playing congas and guitars. I decided to sit on the steps and enjoy my meal and the festivities. The music was great, and the young pilgrims danced until late in the evening. It was an incredible end to a tough day. I climbed into my top bunk and enjoyed the sound of the music and wrote in my journal before drifting off to sleep.

***** *Foncebadon* – *not much to it, but the view from the mountain was spectacular, it was my third favorite view on the Camino behind Orisson and O'Cebreiro*

***** *La Posada del Druida Albergue* – *quaint, friendly owners, nice common area, loved it*

Foncebadon to Molinaseca

12 miles (20km)

This was an exciting day for me. It was a day in the mountains, so I got an early start after packing up and doing feet preparation. I looked forward to seeing the Cruz de Ferro monument.

Everyone seemed to have had the same idea. When I left the albergue, it looked as if every pilgrim in Foncebadon was doing the same. Perhaps, like me, it was the anticipation of getting to Cruz de Ferro. Or it could have been that everyone wanted to get off this mountain as soon as possible. Or perhaps both.

The morning was cool and overcasted, perfect weather for ascending a mountain. Compared to the pilgrims I started the day's journey with, I was still the slowest climber. Whenever time came for me to hike up or down a mountain, I took my time and calculated my steps to avoid a misstep on the loose rocks. I didn't want to agitate my knee or risk falling and sustaining a Camino-ending injury. Many of the injuries I read about occurred descending mountains. I was also concerned that if I were injured since I walked alone most of the time, no one would be there to assist me in a place with no cell phone reception. Again, I was glad that I hiked the extra miles yesterday because the Cruz de Ferro appeared before I knew it.

From my research of the Camino, I knew the Cruz de Ferro was special. It was symbolic, like a spiritual reminder of the purpose and the history of this pilgrimage. The tradition is to place something of value at the base of the tall pole. Many people, so I'd read, place pictures of loved ones, stones, poems and prayers there. This was also a place where many people lay something of significance that represents leaving a burden behind in order to move on from something painful.

There were about ten pilgrims there when I arrived, and each one of us stood and patiently waited for the people before us to have their personal, quiet moment at the monument. Each time a person walked up to take their turn, the person after them, or the person they were with, took precious pictures of them at the monument. It was a beautiful moment for each person. I know it was for me. I had my time, left my momentum and continued on my way. We were at the summit of the mountain and the surrounding views of the mountain ranges and valleys were stunning.

There was a short decent into Manjarin, a tiny village that looked more like a place for free-spirit campers. I saw Arthuro from Puerto Rico and another young American couple I'd talked to a few times. Conversations were limited as we began the long and steep descent. We were at the highest point on the Camino, and the descent was as troublesome as the descent into Zubiri – same dangerous decline, same jagged, slippery rocks. I was grateful for the dry weather because I thought this journey would have been much tougher had there been wet weather.

As if the descent itself wasn't tough enough, the swarm of flies buzzing relentlessly around my head made me almost scream. Until this day, I had never been bitten by a mosquito or noticed a fly. I wondered if it was my deodorant, my soap, or my particular body odor, but the flies wouldn't go away and trying to swat them while using my poles to maneuver my steps was difficult. It was crazy, even comical. Thankfully, I had a neck gaiter in my daypack. I normally wore it to protect my neck from the sun. On this day, I used it to cover my ears to keep the flies out. Now the only fight I had with them was keeping them from getting under my sunglasses and into my eyes. The experience was unreal.

About halfway out of the mountain, there was a food truck where quite a few pilgrims were taking a much-needed break. The young American couple I started the day with took one look at me and started laughing. I had successfully kept the flies out of my ears and my eyes, but apparently, a swarm of them were on my cap and circling my head.

Everyone at the food truck joined the conversation about the annoying flies. The young American husband told everyone that his wife was so annoyed she pulled out her sleeping bag and used it to cover her head. According to the wife, that made her more annoyed since she couldn't hold the sleeping bag over her head and navigate the tough descent. She had to remove the sleeping bag because the descent, she thought, was more important. It was nice to have a moment of pure laughter. It felt good to be silly over something as simple as fighting off flies.

After talking about flies, Cruz de Ferro and the descent, I sat for a while to assess my body, particularly my knee. It didn't feel bad, but I still wasn't done with getting off the mountain. Before leaving the food truck, I changed my hiking shoes for my sandals. The descent caused my toes to press against the front of my shoes. Wearing the sandals freed my toes during the downhill hike.

Much like the descent into Zubiri on Day 3, this day's mountain descent seemed never-ending. It was a beautiful sight though, and I took my sweet time to appreciate the views from the higher elevation.

I met up with a few pilgrims I saw in the last village before Molinaseca. The descent wasn't over, and it made sense to stop for a quick rest break. Thankfully, the further I got off of the mountain, the more I realized the flies were gone. It made me think there must be limited food sources high in the mountain so insects feast on humans or any other living thing they could.

I arrived in Molinaseca happy to have the flies and the descent behind me. Molinaseca was a beautiful village with friendly people, plenty of restaurants and a stream of water at the village entrance, perfect for cooling tired, achy feet.

I had the chance to walk through the village and see the many shops and restaurants en route to the Santa Maria Albergue, located at the far end of the village.

The Santa Marina Albergue was next to a pasture with a group of beautiful horses casually grazing in the sun. The backdrop of nearby mountains was amazing. The cutest little dog greeted me. The terrier yipped at me as I entered. I shared a room with John and his sister Alice, the brother and sister from Georgia. John was still having problems with his feet, but like all pilgrims on the Camino, feet problems were as much a part of the journey as getting from one place to the next – you just did the best you could and moved on.

I sat in the outdoor food area of the albergue with a delicious burger, water and a glass of wine. It was early evening and after the long, tough descent out of the mountains, I wanted – no needed – to relax and cool my tired feet. I walked back to the water stream, sat, and allowed the icy water to dull the soreness. Occasionally soaking my feet was one of the many simple, but wonderful gifts of the Camino.

I ended the evening sharing wine with John and Alice. I asked about Coleen, and neither of them had seen or heard anything about her. I soon went to bed, wrote in my journal and fell into a deep sleep. I was grateful the day was over. It was yet another day that tested my strength and determination

***** ***Molinaseca*** – *beautiful village, highly recommended*

********Santa Maria Albergue*** *– very nice, kind staff, great food*

DAY 27

Molinaseca to Villafranca

19 miles (30km)

I was awakened about 6:00am by the busyness of pilgrims preparing for the day's hike. I felt rested and only slightly sore from the tough mountain descent of the previous day.

I spent a little extra time preparing my feet for the 19-mile (30km) hike to Villafranca. This would be my second longest hike. I was more confident and more physically and mentally prepared than before. The day's trail would be predominantly flat, a nice recovery from yesterday.

My ibuprofen had kicked in by the time I reached Ponferrada. I was surprised how large the city was. It was well-marked with arrows and making my way through it alone was not difficult. I was passing through the beautiful city when I saw a woman walking with her dog. She and I exchanged greetings, and from our brief conversation, I gathered she was American. Curious, I asked and discovered she was from a small town in Texas. Amy had retired and decided, against the wishes of all her family and friends, to leave Texas and move to Spain. She chose

173

Ponferrada after researching possible places to live. This was in her second year, and she was loving every moment of her time here.

Amy said her didn't think twice about selling all her belonging, including her home and packing up a few personal items and her precious dog and moving to Spain. The thought of returning to the states hadn't occurred to her. Other than having to learn the Spanish language, she felt that she fit right in with the Spanish way of life. My inquisitive nature got the best of me, and I wanted to stay and talk more about living in another country. Whenever homesick for family and friends, she Skypes or have them visit her. I wished I had more time, but I still had a good distance to cover, and I needed to move on. Before leaving, Amy recommended that I follow the shady route through the park, and I was happy I did. It was a great, tree-lined route that I would have certainly missed if I had followed the guide. I headed to the trail, happy to have met Amy and learned her story.

I walked along the park trail and thought about how courageous Amy was to leave her established life behind for a new life in a foreign country, where she knew absolutely no one. How bold, particularly since she was 74 years old. The beauty of life – *take risks without knowing the outcome, see how things go*. It was another moment on the Camino, in life, when I knew I was supposed to meet someone with a message that would impact my life. *Take risks and see how things go.*

City dwellings were everywhere during the first half of the day's hike. There were tall multi-unit buildings, power lines, beautiful flowers, even cherry trees. Storks were still plentiful on the Camino since Leon.

I stopped for a lunch break in Camponaraya, about halfway to Villafranca. I passed John and Alice from Georgia soon after leaving the Santa Maria Albergue. John was still experiencing severe pain in his feet, but he remained stubborn and refused to take a day off or transport his backpack to his next destination. Alice had taken the bus a couple of times to deal with her blisters. Their deadline for meeting up with their siblings in Sarria was approaching fast, and the pace to get there in time was getting to them both.

This was an unusual leg of the journey. The first half had a city-feel to it, with buildings, parks, people, and different trail markers that led the way on the Camino. The second half was a return to farmland and vineyards, solitude, and panoramic views of mountains.

It was late afternoon when I arrived in the beautiful village of Villafranca. It was postcard beautiful, one of my favorite stops on the Camino. It was one of the places that I would love to return to someday. It was obviously a popular spot, with large numbers of tourists, residents, and pilgrims.

The Leo Albergue was at the far end of the village close to where the village ended and tomorrow's trail began. Not only was Villafranca one of my favorite places on the Camino, the Leo Albergue was my favorite albergue of all.

The owners, a husband, wife, and daughter were very friendly. After I had checked in, showered and did my laundry, I walked downstairs to the bar for a glass of wine and to find food. First, I decided on a glass of wine; then maybe I thought, I would go out and look around for someplace to eat. I sat at the bar with a man who didn't look like a pilgrim – too clean, too groomed, too relaxed. With my limited understanding of Spanish, I understood enough to learn that he lived nearby and knew the owners. We chatted a bit about American and European politics. Whenever I could, I followed both political situations as I walked the Camino. I checked news channel whenever possible, Facebook and read English newspapers. It was and still is important for me to know what happens with local and worldwide politics. There were important changes going on in my country and in other parts of the world, and no way was I going to ignore them, even while on the Camino. Yet, I had no intention of getting caught up in stressful, back and forth discussions that would do nothing but heighten emotions. After almost four weeks on the Camino, I was protective of the inner peace I'd rediscovered.

While I sat at the bar enjoying the ebb and flow of the Leo Albergue, the wife came out from the kitchen and asked if I was hungry. Of course, I was. She brought me a plate of the best potato salad I'd ever eaten. I mean the best. It was so good that I asked for the receipt. (Tuna, carrots, corn, olives, and potatoes with olive oil). I loved it. I cleaned my plate so fast she smiled and kindly gave me a second helping. The wife and I were talking when the husband chimed in and said it was his favorite dish. I stayed right there for the remainder of the evening – my stomach full and my heart filled from the kindness of the owners.

***** ***Villafranca*** – *the cutest, picture-postcard village*

***** ***Leo Albergue*** – *my overall favorite place on the Camino, cozy, friendly owners, great facility*

Villafranca to O'Cebreiro

18 miles (28.9km)

Last night I slept in a top bunk. This time I didn't mind. I slept well. Realistically, I didn't have any restless nights on the Camino. There were times when a snorer or two, or someone passing me on their way to the restroom woke me, but falling back asleep was never an issue. I'm sure it had to do with the fatigue of covering great distances everyday. Most nights, I was barely able to stay awake long enough to write in my journey after getting into bed. Thirty minutes was enough time to post pictures on Facebook, check emails, contact Javier at Caminofacil about the next location to take my backpack, and to journal. Each night I would lie in bed, read my guide, Antonio's spreadsheet, and decide my next destination. Each night I fought to stay awake to get it all done. If I needed to finish or add something, it was usually done the following morning or evening. But once asleep, I rarely woke before 5:30am. I am not a heavy sleeper. Not at all. So the routine sounds of pilgrims dressing and packing was enough to awaken me. Reading books on my mini-IPAD – as I intended to – never happened while I was on the Camino.

Wrapping my feet each morning helped cushion my feet, so thankfully, I still had a no new blisters, and the old ones were almost healed. I carried my sandals everyday since Burgos after learning that my feet did a lot better when I started the day in my hiking shoes then changed into my sandals usually somewhere around the halfway point. The combination of wrapping my feet, moisturizing them and changing into my sandals was doing the trick.

This would be my second straight 18 miles (29km) day. I took extra care with my feet before heading out on the trail. I needed to get more miles in.

The two helping of potato salad and the one piece of French bread was all I had the night before so my immediate thought was to get food. Today's breakfast was the usual, a café con leche, a croissant, orange juice and a banana. With Antonio's trail mix, I didn't need to buy more food to eat on the trail. I would eat once or twice in passing villages. This day, however, I took an extra banana and two bottles of water instead of one. Not only was this a long hike, but it was also considered one of the toughest legs on the Camino.

I was uneasy about the upcoming ascent into O'Cebreiro, a steep 2300ft (700m) climb. I was nervous. I started to have second thoughts about doing the 18 miles (29km) and the ascent into O'Cabreiro all in one day. Maybe I should have divided this into a 2-day journey.

I was happy at least to see Arturo from Puerto Rico and Tom from Canada as I was leaving Villafranca. It was a fair day: cool, partly cloudy skies, ideal weather for hiking. It called for a jacket and long pants to start the day.

There are three different paths out of Villafranca del Bierzo, all of them with high levels of difficulty. I choose the main route. It was the most level path out of Villafranca. The only major elevation occurred after mile 13 (21k). Just a note. The trail out of Villafranca is adjacent to a major highway. At one point I took a look back and captured a beautiful postcard picture of Villafranca as the sun rose over the lovely village.

At the end of Villafranca was a sign that stated Santiago was (124 miles) 200km away. The feeling of accomplishment was motivating. As I walked, I reflected on how far I had come. I remembered back on day 3 after getting over the Pyrenees how I couldn't wait to have miles and experiences under my belt. Back then, I wondered what it would feel like to have only a hundred mile (161km) to go. In two day, I would know that feeling.

The cool morning felt good, as did walking on a trail with no or very few rocks as I climbed out of the valley of Villafranca. My pace was good, or so it was after my ibuprofen kicked in. It was so good that I walked for most of the morning without my poles.

Arturo was not a fast walker and, like me, he stopped in passing villages for short rests and food breaks. He was either in front or behind me as I walked.

Most of the route crisscrossed the main highway. There were plenty albergues and cafes along this route. I stopped in La Portela de Valcarce. It was my second stop. I watched Arturo, and his hiking partners continue along the trail. It was still early in the morning, the weather was pleasant, and I had no major body ailments, only tired feet. Yet I was worried.

I suspected it this morning, but at this point, I knew clearly that my plan to tackle the climb into O'Cebriero after hiking 13 miles (21km) was not a good choice. I had no idea what I had gotten myself into, and I was concerned. Only a handful of pilgrims were on the trail, and I knew that by the time I walked 13 miles (21km) to the base of the O'Cebriero climb, I would probably be alone. I remained as confident as I possibly could, considering what was to come. I knew that 6 miles (10k) straight uphill would be one of the biggest, if not *the* biggest challenge for me. I looked forward to seeing the incredible views along the Camino, and I didn't want to miss this climb. Taking a taxi was an option. I could also take a mule up, which I seriously considered. I'd seen a couple of signs advertising mule rides to the top. I still had ways to go, and I put the mule idea in the back of my mind for the time being.

I reached the Herrerias Bridge where the three routes merged just before the climb. I passed several stables and decided – right or wrong – to climb on my own, without a horse or mule, and hopefully without a taxi. I was OK with my decision knowing, like on the Pyrenees, taxis up and down the mountains were available, ready to offer rides to any pilgrim in need, for a price of course.

I was tired at the start of the climb. Again, I wished I had stopped for the night in Herrerias, Le Taba, or Logrina de Castilla instead of taking on a 13-mile hike and the climb all in one day. It was a struggle, all of it, but unlike the Pyrenees, I was stronger, much more confident, more of a risk taker. There was no fear, only concern about climbing after an already long day on the trail.

John Brierley's guide made the climb seem like it was mainly straight up. I should have known from the Pyrenees and the climb into the Meseta that the map didn't account for the many switchbacks. To me, this climb was longer but more gradual than the other climbs. There were many switchbacks, and there never seemed to be any leveled road. Thankfully, there were moments of shade provided by the many trees. It was nice to have a snack or water break under a shady tree. I stopped often, but I climbed at a good pace. There weren't many pilgrims on the trail. It was now around noon and I knew it would take the rest of the afternoon to complete the journey. I had reserved a hotel room instead of a bed in an albergue. Having a bathtub would be worth the 35 euros.

I made it finally. It was a long climb, and again, 18 miles (29k) with a 6-mile (10km) uphill hike was not the ideal situation. If I had it to do again, I would hike from Villafranca to La Faba, and from La Faba to O'Cebriero.

I made my way to the Casa Carolo Hotel. All transported backpacks were delivered to a nearby bar. I checked in and found my way to the bar to retrieve my backpack. I sat for a while at the hotel's outside café, taking in the most spectacular view of the mountains. It was stunning.

I went to my room, showered and thought there would be no going back out, but I couldn't rest, and I didn't want to stay in. It was too beautiful outside to be in a hotel room, even one with a great bathtub. I went back out and I spent time in the cathedral, got a stamp in my passport and walked around the quaint village.

Just before starting my ascent into O'Cebriero, I stopped to rest and met a group of five people from Texas. I remembered smiling went I saw them. They were sitting with a pitcher of beer and a bottle of wine laughing and having a festive time. Cleaned and well groomed, I guessed they were just starting out on the Camino. They were. Starting in Astorga, they decided to bus and taxi their way to Santiago. At some point they hoped to walk, but they weren't sure at the time. It was another thing I learned about the Camino. Experience it however you choose. Hike it, bus it, taxi it, take a train, do a combination of them all. There are multiple ways of doing the Camino for anyone wanting to be a part of this great experience.

After leaving the cathedral and walking around O'Cebriero, the group from Texas called me over to have a glass of wine with them. We talked and shared stories about our reason for coming to Spain. The five of them were great friends who often traveled together. Spain and Paris were the destinations for the current 3-week vacation. They were a joyous group, and I was happy to have met and talked with them. I left and went back to the hotel's café where I sat and enjoyed the evening view of the mountains.

Back in my room, I enjoyed another long, hot bath. It was nice to sit in a tub and allow the hot water to relax my sore muscles. I wrote a bit about the day's journey, went to bed and had a restful sleep.

***** *O'Cebriero* – *a beautiful, historical village with incredible views and a wonderful cathedral*

***** *Casa Carolo Hotel* – *very nice hotel, beautiful views*

O'Cebriero to Triacastela

12.9 miles (20.7km)

I went to bed after spending a beautiful evening touring O'Cebriero. One of the hotel staff members recommended that I get up early and watch the sunrise. According to her, the first light over the mountains was breathtaking, and I wanted to see it.

I awoke early enough to repack my backpack and daypack. I walked outside at dawn in time to witness one of the most incredible daybreaks I had ever seen. It was both eerie and stunning to watch the light rise over a thick layer of fog. The mountains looked like islands in a sea of clouds. It is one of my favorite memories of my journey. In fact, many of my favorite photos came from arriving and leaving O'Cebriero.

I dropped off my backpack, had breakfast and started on my journey to Triacastela. After two days of 18 miles, (29km), 12.9 miles (20.7km) – mostly downhill – seemed like a walk in the park. The morning was foggy, almost cold. The easy descent helped my still-tired feet. My knee was a little sore, but no more than usual, nothing that an 800m ibuprofen couldn't take care of. I had trusted my body to grow stronger, and it had. I walked without being winded or feeling the need to puke from fatigue. The sequence of intense mountain climbing on the Camino was over. The remainder of the journey was about managing my time, trying to stay injury free, and enjoying my remaining days on the Camino. And I truly intended to do just that.

I don't care what state a pilgrim is in at this point of their journey on the Camino. It would be hard not to enjoy the beauty of the descent out of O'Cebriero: the mountain range, the thick fog, the rising sun, the greenery. At one moment, I realized that a few weeks ago, I was in an area that was in total contrast. The Meseta was golden, dry, and mostly desolate. The contrasting places were such a metaphor for life. No matter what area of life you are in, it is all about putting one foot in front of the other and moving through it.

I walked alone grateful, truly grateful for the time to myself. Downhills are normally where I would quicken my pace to pick up some time. Not this morning. It was me, my thoughts, nature's beauty, and my nice slow, purposeful pace. It made sense to go easy since my knee became particularly irritated going downhill hikes. This wasn't a steep descent, but it was long, lasting the entire distance.

There were no shortages of villages, cafes and rest area between O'Cebriero and Triacastela. There were six. I didn't stop at all of them, but I did stop twice for a restroom break and to get food. About halfway, I stopped and changed into my sandals. During the last 3 miles (5km) before Triacastela, the descent was slightly steeper. Not bad, just not as gradual as earlier.

Near the end of the descent, I saw a woman sitting near a building with a look of distress on her face. I asked if she was OK. She replied, "Yes." She had the look of pain that I knew too well, so I asked, "Are you sure?" The problem, she finally admitted, was her back. I sat with her and we discussed the weight of her backpack and her destination. We were just outside Biduedo. The next village was Filloval, about 1.8 miles (3k), just beyond the steepest downhill section of the descent from O'Cebriero.

I was concerned about Margaret (I didn't ask where she was from. It didn't seem important at the time). As I sat with her, I realized that sitting with a fellow pilgrim may be the only thing one pilgrim can do for another in a time of need, no matter the situation. All Margaret wanted was a taxi. She had started in Leon and was worried that she'd pushed too hard and the climb into O'Cebriero had taken a toll on her body. Taking a day off had not been in her plans, but the longer we talked the more she began to consider the possibility of taking a day to rest and heal. My one suggestion was to lessen the heavy backpack or transport it for a day or two to take some of the pressure off her back. Before I left Margaret, she asked a local business owner to call a taxi. We hugged and wished each other well.

I loved this part of the Camino. There were sections where trees draped over trails providing much-needed shade. I later came across a father and daughter taking a snack break on the trail. We exchanged greetings. They were from Spain, and this was another of those moments I wished I spoke more Spanish. My basic word knowledge allowed me to survive the Camino, but there were moments, like this one, when I wanted to engage in actual conversations. I wanted to know about the young girl's school life. I guessed her age to be about ten years old. I stopped initially because the father wore a Chicago Bulls hat. It was the second time on the Camino that I'd seen a person from Spain wearing something that referenced my hometown. The first time was in Burgos.

I arrived in Triacastela mid-afternoon. The albergue I chose was on the farthest end of the village. All I wanted was a shower, a short rest, and to find food.

I had gotten savvy with making sure I had a place to lay my head at the end of each day. I still decided the albergue or hotel I intended to stay, and if they had email service, which most did, I emailed my estimated time of arrival.

The previous night I sent an email to the Berce do Camino Albergue requesting a bed and letting them know that my backpack would be delivered. When I arrived, I was told no rooms were available, and the lady in charge wasn't an email person, so she never knew of my request. It was the first time the place where I sent my backpack had no bed available for me.

Not having a bed had been one of my biggest fears. I had read stories about people arriving in villages with no beds only to be forced to hike to the next village. During the first part of my Camino, I had Coleen. We always rose early, and since she was a fast walker, she made it to our chosen albergue hours before I did. I was now on my own. Although I wasn't as slow as before, I still moved at a relatively slow pace compared to most other, younger hikers. I had two things in my favor. One, I traveled solo. Finding one bed was a lot easier than finding two or more. Two, I still started my day early. My goal was always to be on the trail by 7:00am. A couple of days I left a little later, but rarely. Depending on the distance I traveled, I typically arrived at my destination around 4:00pm.

The lady in the albergue allowed me to leave my backpack while searching for a place to stay. She recommended I try the Meson Vilasante Hotel next door. They were able to accommodate me. I paid for a nice small private room and went to retrieve my backpack. After a shower and a short rest, I left in search of food.

I walked through the village, back toward the entrance and found a very nice restaurant where I sat near the entrance and watched the people passing by. There were still a few pilgrims coming in. Although I sat alone, I requested a pilgrims meal because it was steak and salad, bread, custard, and wine. It was delicious. It was the perfect ending to a good day.

***** *Triacastela* – *pretty village, friendly people, beautiful view of the mountains*

***** *Meson Vilasante Hotel* – *friendly staff, small but clean rooms with ample windows*

Triacastela to Ferreiros

21 miles (32km)

I awoke rested and feeling good overall. The descent from O'Cebriero wasn't difficult, and my knee felt no different from any other day after walking downhill. While resting the night before, I made the decision that this would be a good day to add some extra miles. Brierley's guide map recommended a 13.7-mile (22.1km) hike to Sarria. I decided to do 21 miles (32km) into Ferrerios. There would be a slight 492ft (150m) ascent during the final three miles (5k), but it didn't appear too difficult. However, it would be my first time hiking 21 miles (32km).

I was up and out of the hotel by 6:30am. It would be a long day and the earlier I started, the better. There were two popular routes out of Triacastela. Route 1, the San Xil route, had a steep climb that I didn't want to deal with, especially since I was doing 21 miles (32k). I chose the detour route that leads into Samos. It was longer but less hilly.

Hiking next to rivers was still one of my favorite enjoyments. The sights and sounds were calming. There were thankfully many tree-covered paths on the trail that helped make the hike bearable during sunny, hot days. Some of the tree coverings were so thick with overhanging branches that the trails became tunnels. I didn't think about the end of the Camino often, but I knew when it was over, I would miss fellow pilgrims and waking each morning to hike to new locations. But I'd also miss incredible trails with breathtaking scenery and the many flowing rivers, like this day's. This was a long day, and at times I wondered if I had taken on too much. There was no problem with mountains, or rocks, or weather, or pain. Distance was my challenge of the day.

I start noticing more pilgrims on the trail. I knew from reading about the Camino that time was a factor for most pilgrims. Not everyone could sacrifice 35 to 45 or more days away from families or jobs. Most pilgrims who complete the Camino do so in shorter intervals. A good number of pilgirms start in Leon. Even more start in Sarria, a popular starting point for groups of students. I passed through Samos very happy that I had chosen that route. I was able to see the Monastero de Samos, a sixth-century monastery, one of the oldest in the world. I wished I had more time to take a tour. I would love to have seen the monastery firsthand.

There were more pilgrims on the trail the closer I got to Sarria, 11.6 miles (18.7km) from Triacastela. I stopped there for lunch, and because my first passport was now full, I needed to find a new one. I went into a nearby albergue and paid 2 euros for a new passport. Getting stamps in my passport had almost become an obsession and I liked the different stamps. Of course, I always asked for stamps at each albergue and hotel – a requirement for getting a Compostela in Santiago, but I didn't just ask at the places where I stayed. I requested stamps at restaurants, cafes, and cathedrals.

On one hand, I was happy I had chosen not to stay in Sarria. It was a small bustling city, and I preferred smaller towns and villages. Yet Sarria appeared to be the perfect distance, and I was tired. A few times I wished I had stopped there. I took half an ibuprofen and had to dig deep to complete the additional mileage to get to Ferrerios.

On the trail, I met two beautiful young ladies from North Carolina. Dawn and Amber were college students and best friends. They were strong hikers and looked like athletes. The three of us stopped at a restaurant in Morgade, a village just before Ferrerios. Coincidentally, we were staying at the same albergue. Like so many other pilgrims now on the trail, they had started in Sarria. They planned to arrive in Santiago on July 4th or 5th then hike on to Finistere. My plan was to take the bus to Finistere, time permitting.

The scenery and the calming rivers helped take my mine off my tired body. I was ready for a shower and the bed. I arrived in Ferreiros around 5:00pm totally exhausted after almost ten hours on the trail. I checked in and found my bed – happy that it wasn't a bunk. I had to drag my weary body into the shower. As soon as I was done, I returned to my bed and stayed there. I slept for hours, waking one time around midnight to go to the restroom. When I returned, I grabbed two bags of Antonio's trail mix and quickly ate them. Before going back to sleep, I wrote in my journal, posted pictures on Facebook, and emailed Javier at Caminofacil my intended destination for the following day. It was the first and only time I stayed in bed after a day of hiking.

***** *Ferrerios* – *I didn't see much, but it had a beautiful view of the surrounding mountains*

***** *Casa Cruceiro* – *nice and quiet, friendly staff, clean facility*

Ferrerios to Eirexe

15 miles (25km)

I awoke a little sore and still a bit fatigued from the 21-mile (32km) day. And I was hungry. After dressing and packing, I walked to the café next door, dropped off my backpack for transport, and had breakfast. It was about 7:00am. This was one of those times when taking a day off would have been the best thing for my tired body. I wished I could have, but time was a factor, and taking a rest day would have defeated the purpose of the previous day's extra miles.

It had been a while since I had doubts about making it to Santiago in the allotted time. In recent weeks, I'd been feeling good about my chances of completing the Camino de Santiago in time to make my July 6 flight out of Amsterdam.

My body was strong, but I was tired. I knew this day I would require a deeper level of mental fortitude. I needed to do everything I could to squash the self-doubt that kept creeping up. It was a mental battle that would last all day.

Since I'd slept most of the evening and all night, I didn't see the girls from North Carolina, but I did see them on the trail. Like Coleen and I had done when we first started in SJPdP, they too started out together, but separation came fast since one hiked at a considerably faster pace than the other. Again, coincidentally, we were stopping in the same village and staying at the same albergue.

There was a slight ascent at the start of the trail that peaked before a lengthy descent into Portomarin. I was feeling better and happy I was about to deal with a descent instead of a climb. I had intentionally started the day wearing my sandals because of the descent. My feet were fine, and I wanted them to stay that way. Hiking downhill still irritated my toes when they pressed against my hiking shoes. My open-toe Ecco sandals solved that problem. My Ecco sandals were one of the best purchases I made in preparation for the Camino. I still wear them to this day.

The descent into Portomarin wasn't bad. Not until that god-awful, injury-prone boulder trench just before the road into Portomarin. I was on my own, and when I saw the trench, I stood for the longest time wondering if I would be safe going through it. If I slipped on one of the oversized boulders and was hurt, how long would it be before help arrived? It was the most unsafe thing I'd seen on the Camino, and it scared me.

I chose not to go through it. Maybe I would have if someone else had been around. I backed away from the tunnel entry, looked around and decided to walk through the small vineyard next to it. It took climbing up and over a fence, weeding my way through rows of grape vines, and squeezing through ropes used as a fence to get to the road. By the time I made it out of the vineyard, I was dirty – more so than usual –and I was extra tired. I found the whole ordeal comical. I laughed out loud, happy that no one saw me during this moment of insanity, and happier still that I made it out without injury.

I crossed the bridge over the water into beautiful Portomarin. It was postcard beautiful, with a surrounding river, tall trees, hilltop homes, and stunning views. I was only passing through Portomarin, but I decided to stop for lunch and a much-needed rest. I had to first climb up the steep concrete stairs that led to the town. For the past 30 days, I'd climbed up and down hills and mountains and walked over rocks and boulders of all sizes, but the thought of climbing those stairs made me cringe. I held on to the side support and made my way to the top of the stairs. There stood Amber and Dawn from North Carolina talking to another pilgrim.

I found the first outdoor café on the main street, where I sat for the longest time before going inside to buy food, water, and a cold beer. I enjoyed my lunch and watched the few pilgrims as they traveled down the main street. There were a few solo hikers and a group of students with their adult chaperone. After a while, I felt rested and decided it was time to move on. The trail out of Portomarin was uphill, but nothing too steep. It was tree-lined and cool.

I had come to appreciate the libations from the different regions on the Camino. My favorite was the red wines from the Rojas region. Rojas wines were heavier bodied and more flavorful – to me. I was now in the Galicia regions since O'Cebriero, and because the days were hotter, I was enjoying the beers of Galicia. At the end of a long hot day, I wanted a cold beer instead of red wine.

I enjoyed the remainder of the day's hike, appreciating the shade provided by the many trees. The last half of the trail was along the highway. I didn't mind. Although walking adjacent to a highway often meant exposure to the blaring sun, I found it was easier on my feet.

I arrived in Eirexe with several other pilgrims and the girls from North Carolina just ahead. The Airexe Xunta Albergue was at the very end of Eirexe. I checked in and was assigned a bottom bunk next to Amber and Dawn.

Showered and laundry done, I ventured out and found a great café right across the road. With my mini IPAD and Brierley guide, I was excited to sit outside with a delicious queso bocadillo and a cold beer and plot my remaining days on the Camino.

If I remained injury free, I would arrive in Santiago in three days. I found it unbelievable that I had finally made it to this point and that my Camino – this incredible adventure – would soon end.

Though it was almost over, I found that the Camino kept providing experiences that I wouldn't soon forget. Sitting outside the café, I watched a farmer herd cattle on the road right in front of me. The small herd was led to a watering trough next to the café. It was another one of those simply cool things on the Camino.

I spent the evening talking to Amber and Dawn. We laughed about silly experiences on the Camino. We discussed life in general, and one of the best moments of our conversation came when the two of them expressed how they wished their mothers were bold and adventurous enough to do something like hike the Camino. They thought I was brave to do this alone, and at my age. I still smile when I think of the innocent compliment. I never thought of myself as brave. Yes, it was bold and adventurous. It was something I wanted to do. The three of us talked until lights were turned out. It was a good conversation, and I felt fortunate to have met these equally brave young ladies.

***** *Eirexe* – *loved it, simple, friendly residents, good food*

**** *Airexe Xunta Albergue* – *nice and clean, friendly staff, love the location and the café across the road*

DAY 32

Eirexe to Boente

15 miles (25km)

I was up and out of the albergue by 6:45am. Since I enjoyed dinner and people/cattle-watching from the café across from the albergue, it was an easy, convenient choice to stop there for breakfast.

This was a beautiful region of Spain and another beautiful, cool morning. I'd spent so much time on the wide-open Meseta with few or no trees that I kept expecting to see more openness here, but it never happened. The Galicia region was beautiful, full of greenery, and much cooler. The trail was eerie quiet. At one point, I stopped, pulled out my phone and took a picture and a video of the quiet, the stillness. I then made a promise to myself. Whenever the world around me became too distracting with noise and utter nonsense, I would look at the video and pictures of this almost-sacred place. I look at that video from time to time and my fascination of the absolute quietness of that moment on the Camino is recaptured. I thought of this moment as seeing nature's beauty in its simplest state, where less is so much more.

There were small villages along the route where farmers herded their cattle right down the main road. On a few occasions, pilgrims had to stop walking and wait for cattle and farmers to cross from barns to pastures or vice versa.

This was one of the days I thought about Coleen and Antonio. I had met other pilgrims on the trail who I cared about and hoped to see again, but Coleen and Antonio meant the most. I began this journey with Coleen and hoped to see her before it was over. Seeing her on the trail or in Santiago would be the perfect gift to the end of a pretty amazing and meaningful journey. I liked Antonio almost immediately. He was kind, honest and a great hiking partner. He taught me how to survive the Camino. I don't doubt that I would have made it to Santiago had I not met him. But knowing him and having him give me advice and guidance, kept me from having anymore complications. If he hadn't told me about the requirements for getting a Compostela in Santiago, I might have blown my chance. I considered him and Coleen my Camino angels. I would finish without them, but they both helped me learn about the Camino. I don't know what would have happened if Coleen hadn't been there in the beginning to reserve beds for me. I believe life is about growth, and the more I live and experience, the more I grow. I am forever grateful to those who have been there – without selfish agendas – to offer their guidance and support.

I arrived in Boente, a small, older village. Again, the albergue I selected was at the far end. The sight of it had me wondering if I had made the wrong choice. I knocked on the door, and for the longest time, no one answered. I didn't like it that this place was closed. Finally, a man answered and let me in. The first thing I inquired about was my backpack. I followed him through a closed café that smelled stale as if it hadn't been opened in a while. I retrieved my backpack, happy to see two other backpacks there. All other albergues where I had stayed were in full operation when I arrived, even if they weren't yet opened to pilgrims.

I was assigned to a room upstairs over the café. It was a decent room with three bunks. Five minutes later, two ladies – the owners of the backpacks – came in. We acknowledged one other – they didn't speak English, and I was unfamiliar with their language and accent. It was just a guess, but I thought they might have been Slovenian. I showered and unpacked. I didn't do laundry. Food was a priority. I walked back toward the village and found a café and enjoyed a pilgrims meal of steak, fries, salad, and custard with wine. In no particular hurry to return to the albergue, I took out my mini IPAD and Brierley's guide and took my sweet time journaling and planning the next two days. When I returned, the two ladies were already asleep. I got in bed, emailed Javier, then wished for peaceful sleep.

**** **Boente** – *very small village*

* ***Oz Albergue*** – *closed café, unclean, no sheets, older faculty, my least favorite albergue on the Camino*

Boente to Pedrouzo

15 miles (25km)

Of course, I was up and out of the Oz Albergue early. I was on the trail by 6:30am. I couldn't wait. I did sleep well, surprisingly and thankfully. I assumed by the tone of their conversation and the early morning hustle to leave that my roommates were as eager to move on as I was. While dressing and packing, the three of us shared eye rolls and headshakes, strong indications that our sentiments about the place were the same. Ready to leave the experience behind, I waited to have breakfast at a café about a mile beyond Boente.

Perhaps I was more aware of the beauty of my surroundings since I knew my Camino was coming to an end. The day was beautiful and again overcasted and cool. I walked and reflected on my life and my Camino journey. My body – mainly my feet and my knee – was holding up well. I was experiencing the usual muscle fatigue, but nothing out of the ordinary and nothing that a dose of ibuprofen couldn't make better. There were a few climbs that weren't too taxing on my body. Just beyond Burres, I saw Tom from Canada speed by me. He was walking with a deliberate purpose. I didn't ask why. We just exchanged a greeting, and he was gone. Maybe he was on deadline to be someplace at a certain time, or he had an upcoming flight, as I had.

About halfway into the day's journey, I walked through a wooded area, and I could see a guy just ahead standing next to a tree doing leg flexes as if he were trying to loosen his tightened quads. I paused because I was alone, and it didn't feel right. I took my Swiss army knife out of my fanny pack, opened it and held it in my hand. It wasn't fear that I felt. It was caution, a reaction to that uncomfortable feeling in my gut. As I walked passed him, he said, "Excuse me, do you have any change?" I never slowed down. I gave him a firm no and kept going. Again, I never had a problem with letting anyone know that I was watching to see if they were watching or following me. I turned around several times and watched as he continued to do leg flexes against the tree. There was never a moment on the Camino that I felt unsafe. However, I spent most of my journey alone, and being vigilant of everything around me was an important safety measure that I practiced.

I stopped for lunch in Salceda. Amy and Dawn from North Carolina were eating in one of the cafes, so I went in and joined them. We sat together and talked about how each of us was holding up. Luckily neither of us was having any major physical problems. No blisters, no serious knee or back pain. I asked if either of them had seen a man asking for money. They both had. The guy was in the same location. He had asked Amy for money. She told him no and, like me, kept walking. Dawn was close behind and observed the whole interaction. She didn't like the way he looked at her friend as she passed him. As the two of them finished their meal and was preparing to leave, I suggested that stay together just in case 'Mr. Leg Flex' reappeared. I felt they would be safe. It was the final time I would see the girls.

Further on the trail, I passed a wall covered with beer bottles just outside of a café. I laughed at the thought of this idea, perhaps started as a drunken joke by someone at the Casa Tia Delores that had become another Camino landmark.

I arrived in Pedrouzo around mid-afternoon. The weather was slightly overcast and warm, thankfully not hot. I was hungry and tired, yet excited and anxious. I was about to spend my last night on the Camino before heading out to Santiago.

The Cruceiro Albergue was located near the town center, closer to the end of town. A very nice lady who spoke perfect English greeted me. The facility was modern, more so than any albergue I'd stayed at before. There were different levels, and she led me to the basement level and assigned me a lower bunk at the end of rows and rows of bunks. Next to my bunk was a wall of floor-to-ceiling windows with an incredible view of the wide-open patio area and distance mountains. Each bunk was equipped with its own light and electrical strip. The facility was huge, and it was particularly nice not to worry about finding an outlet for my phone, IPAD, and Fitbit. My lower bunk also came with soft white sheets, a pillow and a warm blanket.

After a shower, I hand washed my laundry and hung my items on the clothesline on the far side of the patio. I then went out looking for food. On the main street, I found a café with a bar that served buffalo wings. I never once thought I would eat buffalo wings on the Camino. They weren't on any menu I'd seen before.

I found that at the end a long day of hiking, I didn't want or need a lot of food. I needed to eat for energy, and I needed to hydrate. Whenever I stopped along the trail, I drank water. I drank water as I walked as well. Delighted by the thought of eating a traditional American dish, I ordered the buffalo wings, two bottles of water, and a beer. It was one of my most memorable meals on the Camino. The wings were delicious. And the beer, let me just say, I've been on the hunt to find it, without success, since my return to the States. I'd never heard of radler – a lemon flavored beer – before. Orange flavored yes, but not lemon. I loved it. It was my last night on the Camino, and the great meal and beer was like having a lobster dinner and champagne to celebrate my accomplishments. I only had radler beer this one time, but it became my favorite beverage on the Camino.

The meal was good. I had a great conversation with the waitress and a fellow pilgrim from Canada. I walked back to the albergue and found a very festive group of young people sitting on the patio, laughing, drinking and having a good time. Everyone, in fact, seemed happy. It was the last day for most of us. Some would stop one more time before reaching Santiago. Others would spend a night or two in Santiago before hiking on to Finisterre. Although I didn't know any of the pilgrims here, I felt a kinship to them. We all started the quest to walk the Camino de Santiago. Some in groups, some with a friend or two, others, like myself, solo. It was OK that I was alone.

I retrieved my laundry and went in to pack my backpack for the last time. I emailed Javier at Caminofacil with the name of my Santiago hotel. There were quite a few other pilgrims lying in bed journaling, checking phones, or reading. It was getting late, and after packing, I did my own journaling, posting on Facebook, and checking emails. The night didn't end quietly. The partying and noise outside annoyed several pilgrims. Several times, albergue staff came down to silence the crowd. Personally, I enjoyed them. I thought it is only fitting that the last day on the trail be filled with fun and good times. And yes, there was a fair share of sex going on throughout the night. *Live and let live,* I always say.

***** **Pedrouzo** – *loved it, a great town with plenty of shops and restaurants*

***** **Cruceiro Albergue** – *loved it, great staff, modern facilities, extra conveniences, one of my favorites*

Pedrouzo to Santiago

12 miles (20km)

I awoke with a bundle of emotions and nerves. I was happy, excited and proud that I had come this far. It would be my last day on the Camino. I was anxious and somewhat sad that it was coming to an ending. I couldn't imagine anyone experiencing the Camino for more than a week and not be affected by this very profound experience.

I wanted to arrive in Santiago around noon with the hope of being able to see the pilgrims mass. I was on the trail at 5:30a.m. It was dark, and for the first time I wore my headlamp. This was the only time I walked the trail in darkness. It was a bit eerie, but thankfully, I wasn't alone. There were dozens of pilgrims on the trail. I imagined with the intent of arriving in Santiago early.

The excitement was evident. It could be felt in the cool air of the morning. Everyone walked at a quickened pace, with little or no evidence of fatigue, or dread, or sore knees, or blistered feet. Even I, the slow walker I was, walked with a purpose. I stopped as soon as I could and was happy to sit at a little café in Amenal and enjoy my favorite breakfast of a croissant, café con leche, and orange juice one more time.

I met Marco from Puerto Rico. He was the friend Antonio had told me about. Marco arrived on the Camino two days behind Antonio. He had hoped to catch up with his friend so they could complete the journey together until Antonio had to suddenly return home and help with his injured father. Marco and I talked for a while and left out for Santiago together. We both thought it strange that we hadn't met on trail before this day, especially since he was a good friend of Antonio's, and because we were in most of the towns and villages on the same days. Antonio often talked about the beautiful hiking trails in Puerto Rico, and I discovered Marco often hiked with him.

Like me, Marco had spent most of his time on the Camino alone. He and I talked about our adventures and our home lives. He and Antonio shared their first Camino together. He showed pictures on his phone of the beautiful rainforests in Puerto Rico. He thought I would enjoy the experience of hiking some of its trails. He made it sound appealing. I didn't realize the island had so many nature preserves and rainforests. I hope one day to visit and hike with him, Antonio and Arturo. I shared how much I enjoyed the Camino, that I had never done anything like this before, and that I knew the impact would be everlasting.

The day remained pleasant and cool. As Marco and I made our way to Santiago, I thought fondly of my adventure. Though I'd spent the majority of my time hiking solo, I met Coleen at the beginning, and it was with her help that I acclimated to the Camino almost effortlessly. I met Antonio who made me aware of the rules for getting a Compostelo. And now Marco. I would have been fine walking into Santiago alone, but obviously, it wasn't meant to be that way. And because Marco knew Antonio and Arturo, his company was extra special.

The Camino gave me what I needed, when I needed it. I had heard it said many times throughout my journey *the Camino provides*. From the moment I exited the train in Pamplona and met Coleen, I knew it to be true. Not that I ever doubted it, but I learned to trust that the Camino gives you what you need, when you need it, but you have to trust it.

Marco and I arrived in Santiago about noon. It was a much bigger city than I envisioned. It was bustling with traffic and people, roads and shops. We could see the Praza Obradoiro Catedral off in the distance. We walked mostly in silence, amazed by it all. He, I'm sure, was as tired as I was, but we were both filled with anticipation and excitement as we made our way through the city limits.

We arrived in the plaza and stood in front of the magnificent cathedral overwhelmed by it all. The construction scaffolds didn't diminish the beauty of the cathedral one bit. I had accomplished the dream of most who hope to walk the Camino de Santiago. The plaza was filled with pilgrims and tourist and vendors and musicians. Marco and I took photos in triumphant poses with the cathedral in the background. We were both tired, but we both found our way to the pilgrims office to get our Compostela, the certificate of completion. We were fortunate that only a few people were in line. We were in and out in under an hour.

Once outside the pilgrims office, I saw Tom from Canada and Jai from Hong Kong. With my precious Compostela in hand, I hugged both of them, offered congratulations and left to find my hotel. The Pico Sacro II was thankfully close to the cathedral and I didn't have to walk far. I wanted a bath and to find food, but more than anything I wanted to rest awhile before making my way back to the cathedral for the pilgrims mass.

As I lay in bed resting with my feet up, I had no words to describe how I felt. I wondered for a moment if the feeling was anticlimactic. Did the end of the journey live up to the hype of getting to Santiago and seeing the cathedral? Yes, it did. Santiago and the cathedral were everything I hoped they would be. My problem was it was all ending. Waking each day, walking, passing through beautiful villages and towns, each uniquely different, seeing the vast lands of Spain, saying *Buen Camino* a dozen or more times a day, meeting new pilgrims and seeing familiar faces, enjoying great food, wine and beer everyday, it was all coming to an end.

It is said that it takes 21 days to develop or break a habit. The Camino for me had become a habit, and I knew as soon as I arrived in Santiago that I would miss it. I had come to love, no matter how my body felt, waking each morning and just walking. Walking. Nothing more.

Walking between 5 to 8 hours with only one day of rest. I loved each and every moment of the Camino. It was an experience that taught me more about myself than anything I had ever done before.

My flight from Madrid to Amsterdam was in two days so once in my room, I went online and purchased a one-way ticket from Santiago to Madrid. To ensure I made it to Amsterdam in time for my 12:40pm flight to Los Angeles, I booked a 6:00am flight from Santiago to Madrid, giving me plenty of time to get to Amsterdam. The only problem – though not really a problem – was getting to the Santiago airport on time. I decided to extend my hotel stay and take a taxi to the airport the following night, around 11:00pm. For the first time in my life, I was willingly going to spend the night in an airport.

Travel plans secured, I left the hotel in search of food and to enjoy Santiago. The plaza was alive with pilgrims and tourist. I chose a small pizzeria where I sat and ate a delicious small cheese pizza and had two beers and two bottles of water. The last thing I wanted to do was to be stuck with exchanging euros back to dollars. I wasn't sure of the exchange rate, but I knew it would be costly. After eating, I went out in search of souvenirs for family and friends and a couple of new tee shirts of myself. I had no intention of taking back the clothes I wore on the Camino. With the exception of my hiking pants, hiking shoes, sandals, and outerwear, I'd plan to leave the rest of the clothing.

I dropped off my packages at the hotel and made my way to the cathedral. On my way, I stopped at the taxi stand next to the hotel and inquired about the price for a round trip ride to Finisterre – a place once known as 'end of the world' because early Spaniards didn't know there was land on the other side of the Atlantic Ocean. The cost, according to the taxi driver, would have been 90 euros ($104) for the 51-mile (82.5km) trip there and back. The bus service wasn't an option because of holiday hours. I thought about the cost, and though I wanted to see Finisterre, I decided not to go, but I left the option open with the hope that I would meet up with another pilgrim and share the cost.

I joined about 100 fellow pilgrims in line at the cathedral. I saw a few people I recognized from the Camino, but no one I'd started with. I looked around the plaza, taking in the sights, hoping to see Coleen. I tried to wish her up. Seeing Coleen would have been as meaningful as completing the Camino de Santiago. I was disappointed that I never saw her.

I entered the spectacular cathedral and quickly found a seat as the place began to fill to capacity. As the mass began, I remembered when I made the decision to hike the Camino de Santiago. It was after viewing a segment of Oprah Winfrey's "Belief." I still watch the segment about the Camino on occasion just to see portions of the trail and landmarks I recognize, and to see the pilgrims mass and the beautiful presentation of the Botafumeiro. Seeing the giant golden basket of incense swinging back and forward over the cathedral was amazing. Everyone around had out cell phones and cameras watching and recording the swinging incense burner. So many people remained after the mass basking in the energy and the spirit of people, the mass and the cathedral itself. It would be the final time many of us would see or talk to each other. Some, like me, were flying home or to other destinations in a day or so. Others would hike an additional three to four days to Finisterre.

**** ***Santiago, Spain*** – *incredible city, beautiful cathedral and plaza, very festive, great shops and restaurants*

*** ***Pico Sacro II*** – *decent, small hotel in the plaza, close to the cathedral*

Santiago, Day 2

July 4th is a national holiday in the United States. It celebrates the adoption of the Declaration of Independence in America. I had no idea other countries celebrated it as well.

I left the hotel to find a place to have breakfast. I saw signs of celebration in the plaza. Miniature Spanish flags were being sold, groups were preparing to perform, and musicians were already playing. I found an outside café, sat and watched arriving pilgrims. I saw no one I knew. I watched as men, women, solo hikers, and groups made their way to the front of the cathedral. I looked for Marco but never saw him again. I had expected him to be at yesterday's mass. I later saw Arturo and told him about walking into Santiago with Marco. He hoped to see him before departing the following day.

I walked around for a good part of the day, just enjoying Santiago and the holiday celebrations. I decided not to spend the 90 euros to go to Finisterre. It was a holiday, and the bus schedule would have cut it too close to the time I needed to leave for the airport. I did not want to miss my flight.

I returned to the hotel and removed everything from my backpack. I made two piles, one for the items I would take back with me, and the other for the things I would leave behind. I left my sleeping bag, two tee-shirts (one I'm sure would never be worn again), leggings, my faithful cap, and the silk sleep bag lining. It was time to go. Time to return to life in California.

What the Camino has done for me

The Camino de Santiago is such a metaphor of life. It seems simple. You wake up everyday and put one foot in front of the other to accomplish the task of the day. You plan what you can, yet the simplest thing can often be the most challenging.

The Camino helped me get in touch with my visceral, most authentic self; the self I don't always get to be because of the demands and the busyness of life, and the duties and responsibilities of family, friends, and work.

I experienced pain and learned how to deal with it, how to live with it. I learned to choose endurance over the pain. On the Camino, I chose the quest at hand – to focus on the daily, weekly challenges. To this day, I still do. I will always celebrate the smallest accomplishments in life. And challenges don't scare me. Not living life to the fullest does.

In this book, I talk about blisters and the pain because they were real, and if you plan to hike the Camino de Santiago, understand that pain will be a part of the journey. It was for me and the other pilgrims I met.

But the bigger picture, my reason for hiking the Camino de Santiago and the strong desire to complete it, came from my need to step outside the comfort of all that I had known. That meant enduring the pain and the blisters. It meant being in another country, alone, for more than a month, and conquering my fears.

I saw plenty of people on the Camino who had to leave before they had planned because of injuries, medical reasons, finances, 'snoring' pilgrims, and like Antonio, family issues. I could have been one of them. But, I did it! I made it! I survived with stories to tell and memories that will last me a lifetime. I live with the Camino in my heart, my soul – everyday. I talk about it to whomever wants to hear the story. I still follow Facebook pages, advising, answering questions posed by people thinking about embarking on the journey and doing something outside their comfort zone, as I did.

I can't say enough about my experience on the Camino de Santiago. I wanted something challenging and meaningful. I found that and more on the Camino.

I answered The Call of the Camino de Santiago.

And I am proud to be a pilgrim.

The question my family and friends often asked when I told them about my plan to do the Camino was *Why are you doing it?*

At the beginning of my Camino, during my first pilgrims meal at Orisson, the question most asked was, *Why are you doing the Camino?*

I found that my reason was difficult for some to understand, but my answer to family and friends, and to the pilgrims in Orisson was basically the same. *I'm doing it for the challenge, the adventure, and because The Call to hike the Camino de Santiago was too strong to ignore.*

At the end, after enduring the 500-mile (800km) journey, the question was *Would you do it again?*

From the first time I was asked this question until now, my answer has remains the same. *In a heartbeat.*

In Retrospect

If I had to do it over again based on what I now know about the Camino de Santiago, here are some things I would do differently, what I would advise others to do...

Don't overthink or question the experience. My adventure happened the way it was supposed to happen. No 'what ifs.'

Never take the chance that you will see someone later on the trail. Use apps like WhatsApp to stay in contact with pilgrims you care about. Exchange contact information early, when you first meet them.

Try real hard to stay up late enough to experience the night, moon, and the stars. It's one of the experiences I missed having.

I would wrap my feet from day one. As soon as I started wrapping my heels and toes, the blisters healed, and I never got another one.

I was right to assume I could complete the Camino in 34 days, but it was too rushed. I would take 40 to 42 days next time.

Plan to visit Finisterre. There were other pilgrims who surprisingly had no intention of going. I regret not going.

If you are thinking about hiking the Camino de Santiago, remember that the journey will be filled with obstacles that will seem impossible at times. It is all about persevering beyond the pain, getting to a space where the pain of sore knees and blisters give way to scenery so magnificent, it truly takes your breath away. You will meet people who will enrich your life. I still think about those I met. Don't worry about people who snore. If you are easily annoyed by noisy sleepers, stay in hotels instead of albergues or monasteries. Or get a good pair of earplugs.

Gratitude

My heartfelt gratitude to those who supported my dreams to hike the Camino de Santiago and to write this book. I am forever grateful for your support and encouragement – and sometimes prodding when I needed it. A special thank you to Michael, Cynthia, Monica, Angela, and Caroline for demonstrating true friendship.

To my daughter, LaShawnda. I Love You.

To my Family and Friends on Facebook. You got me through some challenging days. Thank you for the encouraging words.

To everyone I met on the Camino. You made my Camino experience unique and memorable. I will never forget it, nor you.

To the ATT guy who allowed me to post endless photos on Facebook when I was told I could only send a few per day. Thank You.

To Javier at Caminofacil.net +3461079838. Thank you for saving my knee and weary back. You rock!

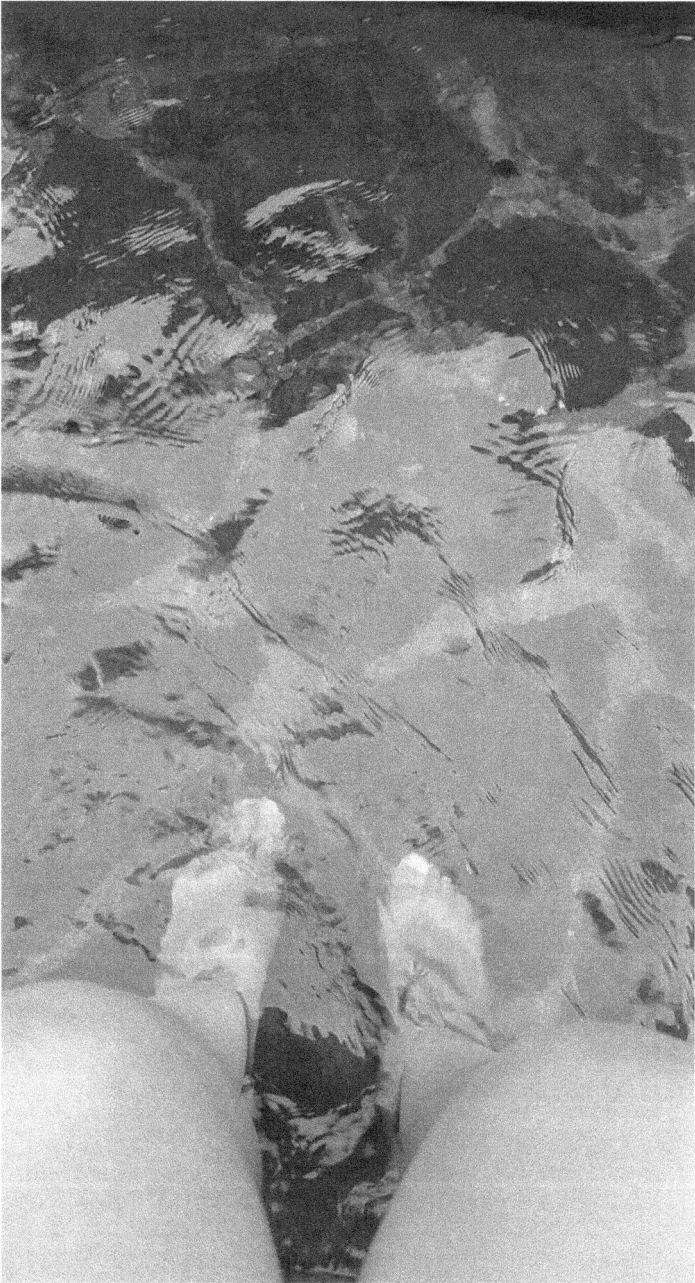

www.ingramcontent.com/pod-product-compliance
Lightning Source LLC
Chambersburg PA
CBHW031544040426
42452CB00006B/174